The History of Conservation
Preserving Our Planet

Reuse It
The History of
Modern Recycling

Ann Byers

Cavendish Square

New York

Published in 2018 by Cavendish Square Publishing, LLC
243 5th Avenue, Suite 136, New York, NY 10016

Copyright © 2018 by Cavendish Square Publishing, LLC

First Edition

Library of Congress Cataloging-in-Publication Data

Names: Byers, Ann, author.
Title: Reuse it : the history of modern recycling / Ann Byers.
Description: New York : Cavendish Square Publishing, [2018] | Series: The history of conservation: preserving our planet | Includes bibliographical references and index.
Identifiers: LCCN 2017027649 (print) | LCCN 2017028538 (ebook) |
ISBN 9781502631275 (E-book) | ISBN 9781502631268 (library bound)
Subjects: LCSH: Recycling (Waste, etc.)--Juvenile literature.
Classification: LCC TD794.5 (ebook) | LCC TD794.5 .B94 2018 (print) |
DDC 628.4/458--dc23
LC record available at https://lccn.loc.gov/2017027649

Editorial Director: David McNamara
Editor: Kristen Susienka
Copy Editor: Rebecca Rohan
Designer: Lindsey Auten
Associate Art Director: Amy Greenan
Production Coordinator: Karol Szymczuk
Photo Research: J8 Media

Printed in the United States of America

TABLE OF CONTENTS

Introduction

Every living creature produces waste. Plants and animals take in what they need to live and grow, process it, and get rid of what they do not use. Waste is a normal and unavoidable by-product of life. In a purely natural setting, one creature's waste is another's nourishment. For example, plants take in carbon dioxide and water, use the carbon dioxide and the hydrogen in the water, and expel the unused oxygen from the water as waste. Animals take in the oxygen, which they need in order to breathe, and get rid of carbon dioxide, which is waste for them and nourishment for plants. As another example, when animals deposit their waste on the ground, it decomposes, releasing chemicals into the soil and the air that feed new plant life. In nature, waste is managed efficiently. It is not really waste, but a resource.

The Three Rs

Ecologists, scientists who study the natural environment, have tried to copy nature's system. They have developed a **hierarchy** of waste management. The hierarchy is known as the three Rs: reduce, reuse, and recycle. It is called a hierarchy because it ranks the steps for dealing with waste in order of priority, from most to least effective. Reducing the amount of waste created in the first

Opposite: In nature, plants, animals, soil, water, and air exist together in balance. Mountain goats eat plants uncovered by melting snow.

The continuous loop of the three Rs symbol suggests that when people implement the hierarchy, they prevent waste.

place is obviously the best way to manage the problem. Reusing a waste product just as it is can keep it from becoming a **discard**, so reuse is the second most effective. If these steps fail, recycling the product, remaking it so it can be used for a new purpose, is also a way to keep waste from simply becoming trash.

The three Rs imitate nature's system for keeping the world clean and healthy. You can see the three Rs at work at the seashore. For example:

Reduce: A gull swoops down, catches a fish, and swallows it whole. By the time the acids in the bird's stomach have done their work, all that is left are a few tiny fragments of bone.

Reuse: A hermit crab fits its soft body into the protection of a shell abandoned by a sea snail.

Recycle: After a growing lobster cracks and sheds its too-small shell, it eats the broken pieces to provide the calcium that strengthens its new shell.

Humans and the Three Rs

People have not been as successful as nature in implementing the three Rs. By the time the first Earth Day spotlighted the issue of pollution in 1970, Americans were producing 3.25 pounds (1.47 kilograms) of solid waste per person every day. Plus, they were tossing 93 percent of it into **landfills**, trash heaps that blighted the countryside. Much of it ended up on city streets and in lakes and rivers. However, the Earth Day activities, together with similar events in several other countries, garnered international concern. The result was an environmental movement.

It was not the first environmental movement, nor would it be the last. At different times, people concerned with **ecology**, the relationship between living things and their environment, brought people's attention to environmental perils. The various movements focused on different issues: conservation, pollution, depletion of resources, hazardous materials, **greenhouse gases**, and global warming. Government leaders as well as scientists and ordinary citizens have addressed the problems these issues have raised.

Before the 2016 Rio de Janeiro Olympics, workers tried to clear waterways of trash and sewage that had accumulated for decades.

At the heart of every issue was one common factor: waste. Waste appeared in many different forms—litter strewn on roads and floating in oceans, sludge left at mining sites, exhaust from cars and trucks, smoke and fumes from industrial furnaces. Land, water, and the air were being devastated because people were not dealing responsibly with their waste. The various environmental movements sought to find ways to eliminate, or at least reduce, the waste.

Reducing Waste

The easiest place to start was at the bottom of the waste management ladder, with recycling. First, laws were passed that set limits on how much waste factories could spill into rivers and streams and spew into the air. Then rules were made for what could be done with solid and hazardous wastes. Recycling mills sprang up that turned bottles, aluminum cans, and waste paper into new bottles, cans, and paper. As cities offered curbside pickup of these items, recycling became popular and fairly widespread. A huge industry grew around the collection, sorting, distribution, and processing of recyclable articles.

Recycling alone would never be enough to rid the land of waste, however. Not everything was recyclable. Solutions would have to be found higher on the waste management hierarchy, with reduction. How could society reduce the amount of waste created in the first place? Manufacturers became responsible for designing products with less waste. Energy-efficient appliances and cars with high gas mileage are examples of their success.

Designing for less waste is a step toward a cleaner environment, but the goal of the modern environmental movement is sustainability—preserving Earth and its resources so they can continue to support future generations. Any waste at all is a threat to that vision because some of what is wasted cannot be replaced. Today's environmentalists are moving toward a goal of a zero-waste society. In that society, recycling is close-looped. That is, any waste from one product or activity becomes the raw material for another. Some companies are already coming up with innovative ways to turn the discarded parts of their products into new items.

We know the three Rs work. We see them functioning in nature. However, for them to work in society, people have to intentionally put them into practice. In some countries, where recycling is encouraged and simplified, nearly two-thirds of the population recycles. In others, almost nobody bothers to recycle. The people living where recycling rates are high are rewarded with clean and pleasant cities, thriving parks and wilderness areas, safe drinking water, and healthy air. Perhaps more important, they know their children and grandchildren will also be able to enjoy these things. That, after all, is the purpose of waste management.

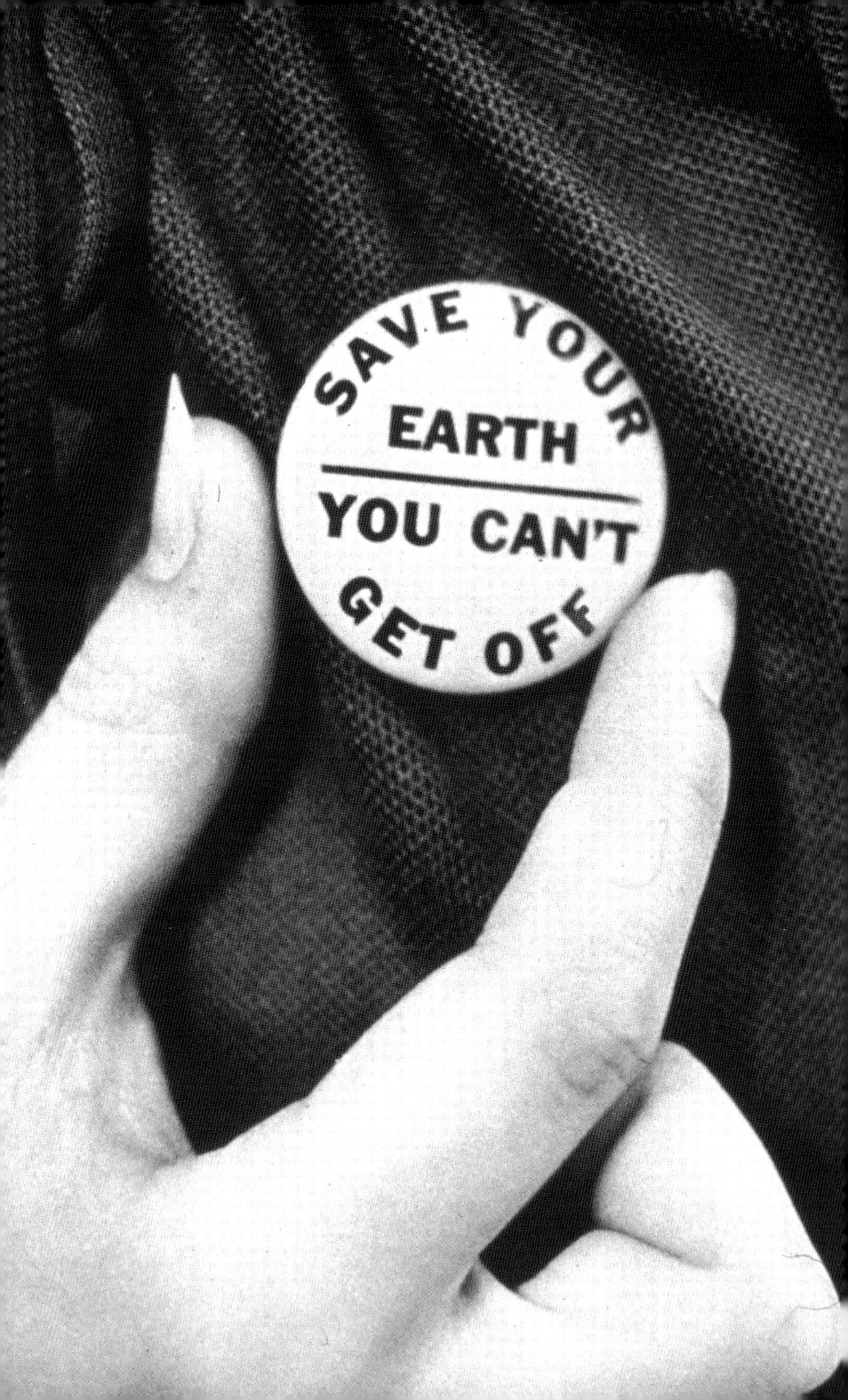
SAVE YOUR
EARTH
YOU CAN'T
GET OFF

1

The World Wakes Up

The practices of reusing and recycling have been around as long as humans have been on the planet. For centuries, people have reused their possessions, not out of a concern for their environment, but because they had little choice. Before the Industrial Revolution, when everything was handmade, people did not have the raw materials or the time to make or buy something new when the old object wore out. They mended their shoes, patched their clothing, and melted metal objects to make tea kettles and rifles. They didn't think of these activities as recycling, but as making do with what they had.

In a preindustrial rural economy, there was little waste to manage. Kitchen scraps were fed to pigs, and anything that could not be used was buried. But as Western Europe and North America became industrialized, people moved from farms to cities. The increasingly crowded urban areas had no place where

Opposite: Organizers of Earth Day 1970 created buttons like this one in the hope that people would continue to conserve.

discards could be buried and not enough animals to eat food scraps. Garbage was either thrown into rivers or dumped in streets and alleys. The cities of the 1700s and 1800s were dirty, smelly, disease-ridden places. Even the White House was infested with rats and cockroaches.

Some cities found creative approaches to dealing with the trash. Charleston, West Virginia, passed a law barring anyone from shooting the vultures that helped clear its streets of food waste and dead animals. Washington, DC, sent its garbage down the Potomac River on barges. When people in Alexandria, Virginia, spotted the barges, they sank them before they could reach their shores. New York City found the most effective solution for the times; in 1885, an incinerator was built on Governor's Island to burn the refuse. Other cities soon followed suit, and within twenty years, 180 incinerators were operating throughout the country. So the earliest public, or government, policy for waste management was to bury it or burn it. No reuse or recycle—just get rid of it.

Money in Trash

However, resourceful people saw value in some of the garbage. Rags could be sold to paper manufacturers, and bones could be used as fertilizer. Some items were snatched up by peddlers, who loaded them on horse-drawn carts and traded their wares from place to place. Thus the profit motive—the desire to make money—led to private recycling or reusing efforts.

One of the first neighborhood recycling programs was also motivated by an economic interest. The Salvation Army, which came to the United States and Canada from England in the late 1800s, was concerned with the plight of many who had no jobs. The Army organized Household **Salvage** Brigades. The brigades collected paper, bottles, furniture, and other unwanted items from homeowners and sold what they could. The materials were called salvage, meaning saved from destruction. But the real reason for the recycling was to save the unemployed from poverty. The leaders of the organization said the enterprise supplied "a maximum of work at a minimum of cost."

Gradually, others realized that salvaged materials were worth money. When people discovered they could make new paper from old more cheaply than from rags, a market for used newspapers opened. Baltimore, Maryland, started curbside pickup of newspapers in 1874 to take advantage of that market. Manufacturers also learned that aluminum could be recycled over and over. In 1904, aluminum recycling factories made their debut in the United States: one in Chicago, Illinois, and one in Cleveland, Ohio.

fact!

There is no limit to the number of times aluminum can be recycled. A recycled aluminum can is usually back on the shelf as a new can within sixty days.

The White Wings

As cities grew, private efforts spurred by small monetary gains were not enough to clear the streets of the heaps of waste that accumulated. The filth bred diseases that claimed many lives. The city of New York took action in 1895. The mayor called on Colonel George Waring to take charge of the city's fourteen-year-old Department of Street Cleaning (after Theodore Roosevelt turned the job down!).

Waring, a Civil War veteran, approached his new position with military rigor. He organized his ragtag army of three thousand street sweepers into an efficient force. He outfitted them in crisp white uniforms and white helmets. The uniforms symbolized their mission; they were to make the streets as clean as their spotless clothing. The uniforms' resemblance to doctors' jackets helped people associate cleanliness with health. The helmets, like those of soldiers and police, gave the men an air of authority. The people of New York nicknamed them the White Wings. Colonel Waring called them "soldiers of cleanliness and health."

Part of Waring's reform of the Department of Street Cleaning was the establishment of the first large-scale government recycling program in the United States. New York City residents were required to separate their trash into three categories: ash from their fireplaces, food waste, and everything else. The ash was used as landfill, mainly to expand Rikers Island in the East River. The grease and oil from food waste were sold as fertilizer or ingredients for soaps. The remaining rubbish was taken to picking yards, where it was sorted into various grades of paper, bottles, carpet, twine, horsehair, and so on. Waring reported that the sale of these items netted the city at least $140,000 per year initially. He predicted that this recycling would eventually cover at least half the cost of his army of White Wings.

Economics and Patriotism

Within a decade or two, other cities adopted street-cleaning programs similar to those of New York, but few established picking yards. The huge amount of labor they required was not practical for smaller cities with less trash. For a time, some burned the refuse, but the incinerators were often abandoned as nearby residents complained of the smoke and the smell. The most common method of managing waste was to simply dump it somewhere out of sight. The United States still had vast tracts of unused land and seemingly endless rivers.

In the early twentieth century, New York City's army of street cleaners
kept the city's streets clear of snow as well as trash.

The volume of waste grew as the country became more prosperous. Most people no longer had to patch and reuse worn items; they simply bought new ones and threw out the old. However, hard times revived the practice of recycling. During the Great Depression of the 1930s, many people were out of work and could not purchase even basic items. Women made dresses from flour sacks, wove strips of threadbare sheets into blankets and rag rugs, and turned the legs of their stockings into hats. They could not afford to waste anything.

When the demands of two world wars depleted resources at home, government campaigns urged citizens to save used paper and tin foil, old tires, rags, and other items they would otherwise throw away. Prominently displayed posters told people that "half the metal in every ship, every tank, every gun is scrap." Families gladly contributed aluminum cooking pots and metal toys to be recycled into airplane parts and cooking fat to be used in making bombs. Schools and companies had contests, and cities established collection sites. Historians question just how much the tons of salvaged materials actually helped on the battlefront, but the recycling drives kept up enthusiasm for the war effort.

Throwaway Society

Patriotism aside, the main driver of recycling through the first half of the twentieth century was its monetary value. When it made economic sense or met a financial need, people took cans to a recycling center or picked through garbage for items to sell. When profit was to be made, companies paid for returned bottles or melted scrap metal to make new cars. If there was no financial gain, waste was burned or tossed into trash yards.

After World War II, in the 1950s, reusing discards had little to no value for most Americans. City trucks picked garbage up

A Gas Mask requires 1.11 pounds of rubber

A Life Raft requires 17 to 100 pounds of rubber

A Scout Car requires 306 pounds of rubber

A Heavy Bomber requires 1,825 pounds of rubber

America needs your
SCRAP RUBBER

This World War II poster encouraged Americans to take old tires, hoses, rubber shoes, gloves, and raincoats to recycling centers.

regularly, so people paid no attention to their trash. In fact, they created more of it. The August 1, 1955, edition of the popular *Life* magazine featured an article titled "Throwaway Living" that actually encouraged wastefulness. The subtitle, "Disposable Items Cut Down Household Chores," praised the virtues of the single-use plastic container. Instead of spending time cleaning plates, diapers, or any number of common items, the article suggested, just use them once and throw them away.

But where would all the disposables go when their usefulness ended? Many never made it to a trash can. Streets, highways, parks, and public areas became littered with the throwaways. The rest ended up with all the other garbage at city dumps. At first, these disposal yards were just what the name implies: open spaces where all the refuse from a city was dumped. At the end of every day, or at least periodically, they were set on fire to make room for more garbage. Of course, everything did not burn. The new plastics, especially, sent plumes of toxic smoke into the atmosphere.

By the 1950s, engineers had found a better way to manage the waste. City workers compacted, or squeezed down, the mounds of trash every day and covered them with fresh dirt. These actions helped control the odor and the flies, but they created other problems, less obvious but more serious. The garbage rotting under the layers of earth released gases. Some of the gases occasionally escaped through the dirt and erupted in fires. The rest seeped into the groundwater beneath the disposal yard. That groundwater, with its toxic pollutants, made its way into streams and rivers, drinking water supplies, and people's homes. These issues did not come to public attention until the environmental movement of the 1960s and 1970s.

Where Does the Waste Go?

What happens to municipal waste? It is recycled or **composted**, incinerated, or landfilled. The chart below shows how several countries treated their municipal waste in 2013.

Country	% recycled	% incinerated	% landfilled
Germany	65	35	0
Japan	19	77	1
Austria	58	35	4
Korea	59	25	16
France	38	34	28
United Kingdom	43	21	34
Ireland	40	18	42
United States	35	12	54
Poland	29	8	63
Canada	24	4	72
Greece	19	0	81
Mexico	5	0	95
Chile	1	0	99
Turkey	1	0	99
New Zealand	0	0	100

Source: Organisation for Economic Co-operation and Development

Dead Birds and Burning Rivers

Some people had noticed the damage throwaway living and other careless actions were doing to the environment, but they had difficulty getting others to see how serious the problem was. One of the first people to break through the disinterest was Rachel Carson. A marine biologist, Carson had written articles and books about sea life. Two of her books had been best sellers. Carson used her popularity as a prize-winning author to alert the world to the harm people's irresponsible behavior was doing to the natural environment she loved.

The topic for her new book was the pesticide DDT. A powerful insect fighter, DDT often killed more than the bugs it targeted. A friend had told Carson that large populations of birds were dying near fields sprayed with DDT. Carson looked into the friend's claim and found that not only birds but other animals also were being affected by the pesticide. In fact, DDT was getting into the food supply, not just in the United States but worldwide, causing cancer and other diseases. After four years of painstaking research, Rachel Carson published *Silent Spring* in 1962.

The book did more than expose the dangers of DDT. It showed that the planet was fragile, that people could and often did upset the delicate balances in nature, and that the consequences could be disastrous. Carson pointed out that if people did not protect the natural environment, the forces of industry were likely to destroy it. She warned that a poisoned environment would eventually poison people.

Silent Spring was an overnight success all over the world. In its first year, it was translated into seven languages, and in the next years into ten more. As of its fiftieth anniversary in 2012, it had sold more than two million copies. Portions

From childhood, Rachel Carson loved both nature and writing. Here, she studies nature near her home in 1962.

were reprinted in popular magazines and read over the radio throughout Europe. Although hers was not the only voice raising the alarm about pollution, Rachel Carson is often seen as the first spark of what became the global environmental movement of the 1960s and 1970s.

In addition to concerns over pesticides, two environmental catastrophes fueled the environment movement. One is known as the Lake Erie fire, although it was actually on the Cuyahoga River where it empties into the lake, near Cleveland, Ohio. The river was a convenient place for the steel mills and other plants that lined its shore to dispose of their industrial waste. Decades of dumping had grossly polluted the waters of the Cuyahoga and several other rivers. Every now and then the sludge in the Cuyahoga, as well as in the Chicago, the Buffalo, and Michigan's Rogue River, erupted in flames.

The Cuyahoga had burned at least thirteen times before the June 1969 fire. That fire was not the largest or the most costly. It was barely even mentioned in the local newspaper. However, it was reported a month later in *Time* magazine. The widely read article focused on the river's pollution, saying the water "oozes rather than flows." Above the story was a dramatic photo of the river ablaze, which was actually a picture of a far more disastrous fire seventeen years earlier. The picture, together with the story, was enough to convince an already concerned public of the need to clean the nation's waterways.

Death in the Ocean

Americans were already aware of the destruction contamination could bring to their waters. Six months earlier, in January 1969, they had witnessed what was at that time the largest oil spill in the ocean. (Today it is the third largest.) Workers drilling for oil 6 miles (10 kilometers) off the coast of Santa Barbara, California, had a blowout; pressure from the natural gas blew a hole in a pipe. Over the course of eleven days, the rupture released 200,000 gallons (757,082 liters) of crude oil into the Pacific Ocean. The wind and waves carried the oil over 800 square miles (2,000 square kilometers). At least 35 miles (56.3 km) of the California coastline and parts of four islands were covered in the black tar.

The pictures that flooded newspapers and television screens in the days and weeks that followed woke people to the horrors human activity could inflict on the natural surroundings. The oil killed fish and other marine animals, dolphins, sea lions, and more than 3,600 birds. The stench from the oil hung over the seaside communities for months. An outraged public did more than gasp and complain. Residents of coastal towns spread straw on the beaches to absorb the oil. Scores of volunteers tried to rescue dying birds and clean the tar from their feathers. Over one hundred thousand people signed a petition to put a stop to drilling off California's shores. More than any other event, the Santa Barbara oil spill mobilized ordinary citizens to do something to clean and preserve the environment.

Igniting a Movement

One of those citizens was Gaylord Nelson, a senator from Wisconsin. Nelson was not a newcomer to environmental causes. Earlier, as governor of Wisconsin, he had created public parks and wilderness areas so portions of the state would be free of traffic and buildings. He had started a Youth Conservation Corps that employed young people to develop the green spaces and keep them clean and natural. His popular programs earned him

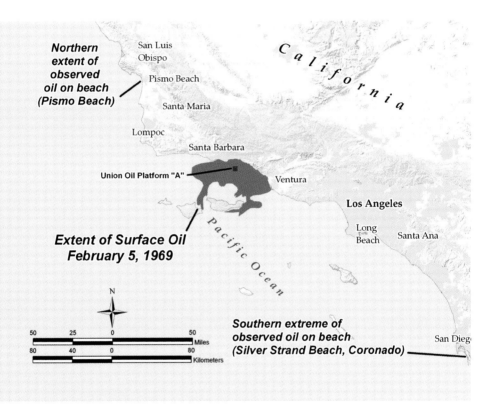

Northern extent of observed oil on beach (Pismo Beach)

San Luis Obispo

Pismo Beach

California

Santa Maria

Lompoc

Santa Barbara

Union Oil Platform "A"

Ventura

Los Angeles

Extent of Surface Oil February 5, 1969

Pacific Ocean

Long Beach

Santa Ana

N

50   25   0   50
Miles
80   40   0   80
Kilometers

Southern extreme of observed oil on beach (Silver Strand Beach, Coronado)

San Diego

This map shows where oil lingered more than a month after the Santa Barbara disaster, from California's central coast to San Diego.

a reputation as the conservation governor and helped get him elected to the US Senate.

In the Senate, Nelson tried to interest his fellow members of Congress in environmental issues. He proposed national programs and legislation that would preserve parks, safeguard rivers, restore forests, and protect wildlife. However, no one in the federal government seemed concerned about conservation.

So, Nelson looked elsewhere. As he watched the news coverage of the Santa Barbara oil spill, he noticed that many of the people taking positive steps to deal with the disaster were students in the college town. At that time, college students were very involved in national issues, protesting the war in Vietnam, for example, and marching for civil rights. They were energetic and idealistic. If Nelson could direct some of that energy and idealism, he might be able to ignite a movement among college students. That movement, if it were big enough and loud enough, could call attention to the need to care for the environment. Other people would have to notice, particularly politicians, and they might feel pressure to do something about preserving the environment.

Nelson announced a national "teach-in" on the environment. Some of the Vietnam War and civil rights protests were sit-ins, during which people occupied an area and refused to move. Because it sounded like sit-in, the term "teach-in" appealed to young people. At the same time, the "teach" part of the term kept it from sounding like a protest. Nelson really wanted to educate people about conservation measures they could take. He scheduled the event at what he hoped would be a good time for college students: during a lull between spring break and final exams. He enlisted a congressman and a graduate student at Harvard to help organize and promote it.

Tying Human and Environmental Survival Together

In Canada, as in the United States, the 1960s saw a counterculture movement, a push to go against the established norms. One of those norms, in the middle of the Cold War, was the testing of nuclear bombs. Another, born of affluence, was disregard for preserving the environment. Reactions against these two norms met in the countercultural organization Greenpeace: "green" for the concern for the environment, and "peace" for the aversion to weapons of war.

The issue that brought the two concerns together was the United States' testing of nuclear bombs on Amchitka Island, between the mainland of Alaska and the Soviet Union. A 1969 underground test had set off earthquakes, triggered mudslides, killed wildlife, and churned the ocean for miles. Radiation seeped from the blast site into lakes and streams. Thousands of Canadians had demonstrated to try to stop the test, but to no avail. Despite the protests and the ecological damage, the United States announced plans for another test, of a bomb five times more powerful.

Warning that such an explosion could create a massive tidal wave, a protest group formed, calling itself the "Don't Make a Wave Committee." The small band of environmentalists, pacifists, and journalists had a plan to stop the nuclear testing. They would sail to Amchitka and refuse to move. Surely no one

Volunteers load the fishing boat *Phyllis Cormack*, renamed *Greenpeace*, for the 2,484-mile (3,000 km) trip from Vancouver to Amchitka Island.

would unleash a 5-megaton explosion with a dozen civilians in the direct path of any tidal wave. Through a rock concert and a media campaign, the group raised enough money for an old fishing boat. Renaming both their organization and the boat Greenpeace, they set sail from Vancouver on September 15, 1971.

They did not succeed; the blast went off as scheduled. However, the publicity the voyage generated sparked widespread opposition to the program, and the United States scrapped the tests that had been planned. From that small beginning, Greenpeace has grown to become one of the largest and best-known organizations dedicated to protecting the environment and promoting peace. It is international in scope, headquartered in Amsterdam, with offices in more than thirty countries.

The Movement Succeeds

The teach-in on April 22, 1970, came to be called Earth Day. It succeeded beyond even Senator Nelson's expectations. An estimated twenty million Americans gathered in high school and college auditoriums, spilled out into streets, and poured into parks all over the country. They held marches, rallies, and demonstrations. They lamented the pollution of streams, the scarcity of green spaces, the spewing of factory smoke into the air. They demanded that elected officials take action to protect the environment.

Politicians heard the cry, which was loud and clear. The first Earth Day was followed by a flurry of environmental legislation. The Clean Air Act (1970) regulated emissions of pollutants from factories and cars. The Clean Water Act (1972) set quality standards for waterways, limiting the flow of raw sewage into lakes, rivers, and streams. There would be no more burning rivers! The Endangered Species Act (1973) protected both plants and animals that were threatened with extinction. The Resource Conservation and Recovery Act (1976) made rules for safe disposal of solid and hazardous waste. A host of other laws shielded people and the environment from toxic chemicals and harmful practices.

Of all the federal action in response to the first Earth Day, the biggest and most far reaching was an executive order issued by President Richard Nixon. The order, which took effect December 2, 1970, established the Environmental Protection Agency (EPA). The EPA was and remains the federal body that ensures that all the laws pertaining to the environment are enforced.

Another long-lasting legacy of the first Earth Day came from a contest sponsored by the Container Corporation of America.

The company made boxes from recycled paper. The company's executives wanted to encourage the growing public interest in environmental issues and advertise its products as environmentally sound. They invited college graphic art students to design an image to represent recycled paper. The company would place that image on its products that were either made of recycled paper or could themselves be recycled. From more than five hundred entries, the executives selected the design of University of California, Los Angeles, student Gary Dean Anderson.

Anderson's submission was a simple drawing: three arrows, each bent in the middle, forming a triangle. The arrows, sometimes called "chasing arrows," make a continuous loop that is meant to suggest that an item can be used over and over in the same form or as something new. That image, unveiled as part of the 1970 Earth Day activities, has become the international symbol for recycling. Over the years it has been modified slightly, and numbers and words have been added for specific purposes, but the symbol itself has remained basically unchanged. It can be seen today on millions of products in countries all over the world.

A Cleaner Environment

Earth Day 1970 is often said to mark the birth of the modern environmental movement in the United States. The first environmental movement, in the late nineteenth and early twentieth centuries, had been about conservation, about preserving land and wildlife. The second environmental movement focused on pollution, on ridding the air, water, and ground of litter, toxic chemicals, and industrial waste. Earth Day awakened the nation to the fragile condition of the natural world and rallied ordinary citizens to do something about it. It brought attention to human causes of environmental peril.

The shift in focus was obvious not only in clean air and water laws, but also in everyday life. To mark the first anniversary of Earth Day, in 1971, the Keep America Beautiful organization released a one-minute public service television ad. It featured actor Iron Eyes Cody (who was actually Italian American!) as a Native American silently paddling a canoe past factories belching smoke across the sky. Just as he beaches the canoe on the trash-strewn shore, a car drives by and garbage tossed from the window lands at Cody's feet. The camera zooms in on his face and a tear spills down his cheek.

Known as the Crying Indian ad, the television spot, repeated many times, did more to reduce littering than any legislation. Five months later, the US Forest Service launched a campaign to keep its parks free of unsightly trash. It introduced a new antipollution icon named Woodsy Owl with the slogan "Give a hoot—don't pollute!"

fact!

Recycling one glass bottle saves enough energy to keep a 100-watt lightbulb burning for four hours.

The emphasis on a clean environment led naturally to an interest in recycling. An energy crisis in 1973 heightened that interest. During that crisis, the supply of energy-providing oil dropped precipitously, and the price rose sharply. Reusing and recycling glass and metal not only reduced litter, they also saved energy.

In the 1970s and 1980s, several cities began offering curbside pickup of recyclable products alongside normal garbage collection. Homeowners started composting, plowing their food and lawn waste into the soil of their gardens. Some US states and Canadian provinces passed "bottle bills" that required beverage companies to refund a small amount of money to consumers who returned their glass bottles for recycling.

However, progress was slow. Recycling took time and was not always convenient. Most people did not see the direct impact of wasteful habits on the environment, nor did they understand the cost of throwaway living. Without something to keep people focused on the need and value of recycling, the practice waned. Some people thought what was needed to kick recycling into high gear was another Earth Day.

One of those people was Denis Hayes, the Harvard student who had helped create the 1970 campaign. He put together a network of concerned environmentalists to organize a celebration of the twentieth anniversary of the first Earth Day. He hoped it would be big enough to mobilize the kind of enthusiasm that would make a real difference.

Earth Day 1990 was twenty times larger than Earth Day 1970. At least two hundred million people in 141 countries participated. The day reinvigorated and broadened the environmental movement and fueled global interest in recycling. It began a discussion on environmental issues that continued through the decade and into the twenty-first century.

2

Nations
Take Action

International interest in Earth Day 1990 was sparked by a series of environmental disasters. The catastrophic events occurred all over the globe. In 1984, a leak at the Union Carbide pesticide plant in Bhopal, India, spewed toxic gases and chemicals into the atmosphere. The worst industrial accident in history, the Bhopal incident poisoned more than half a million people. Two years later, an explosion in a nuclear reactor near Chernobyl in Ukraine sent radioactive clouds over much of Europe. In 1989, the tanker *Exxon Valdez* spilled nearly 11 million gallons (41,639,529 L) of oil into the waters off Alaska. This was more than fifty times what had been spilled in the Santa Barbara disaster. Four months earlier, the *Odyssey* had dumped even more, 40 million gallons (151,416,471 L), near the coast of Nova Scotia.

These and other environmental calamities drew attention to three important realities. First, people could and did cause

Opposite: This debris, found on a Hawaii beach, came from the Great Pacific Garbage Patch, a huge mass of trash in the Pacific Ocean.

significant damage to air and water—all four incidents were results of human error. Second, economic activity had impacts on the environment; each disaster was connected with some business enterprise. Third, events in one country affected people in other nations. Global concern over these disasters, spotlighted by the thousands of Earth Day rallies, led to international action.

A Global Environmental Agenda

The United Nations called its member nations together to tackle the large environmental issues facing them all. The conference, held from June 4 to June 14, 1992, in Rio de Janeiro, Brazil, was the first large-scale international conversation about the environment in twenty years. Earlier meetings had established principles, frameworks, and structures for environmental action, but the conference in Rio had an urgency that produced commitments for international cooperation on those actions. In attendance were representatives from 172 countries. Of these, 108 were heads of state—that is, they were presidents, prime ministers, and other leaders. The presence of these powerful people showed how important taking care of the environment had become. In addition to government officials, thousands of people representing private organizations were also part of the conference.

Because of its emphasis on preserving the environment, the Rio conference was popularly known as the Earth Summit. Its official name was the United Nations Conference on Environment and Development. The title reflected the belief that development was tied directly to the environment.

"Development" is a term that means the economic growth and well-being of countries, societies, and individuals. Countries and individuals nearly always want to grow economically, but sometimes that development comes at the expense of the environment. For example, people might cut down trees in a particular valley and use the wood for economic development—say, to build houses to make their lives better. But if they cut all the trees, they damage the valley's environment. The valley no longer has trees, the animals in the valley do not have the food or homes the trees provided, the grass withers because it has no shade, and on and on.

The United Nations conference used the phrase "**sustainable development**," meaning activities that bring growth today without using up resources that might be needed tomorrow. Sustainable development is progress that can be sustained, or kept up. It balances economic growth with environmental conservation. In the example above, if the people building wooden houses in the valley (economic growth) planted a sapling or two for every tree they cut down (environmental conservation), they would be practicing sustainable development. The generation that came after them would have trees.

The main accomplishment of the Earth Summit was an action plan for sustainable development. It was called Agenda 21 because it laid out goals to be achieved in the twenty-first century. Delegates from all 172 countries as well as representatives of the organizations at the conference agreed to work together to help everyone reach the goals.

The Big Issue

Agenda 21, which is still being followed today, is an ambitious program with substantial goals. Its forty chapters detail programs for protecting the atmosphere, oceans, fresh waters, forests, and all kinds of plant and animal life. It deals with broad topics such

UNITED NATIONS CONFERENCE ON
ENVIRONMENT AND DEVELOPMENT

Rio de Janeiro 3–14 June 1992

This image shows some of the nations of the United Nations joining together at the Earth Summit in 1992.

as climate, energy, chemicals, trade, agriculture, industry, and poverty. It calls for safety measures that would prevent tragedies such as Bhopal.

Of all the concerns at the conference, one issue loomed especially large. It was prominent in all the meetings and throughout the entire text of Agenda 21. Whether the discussion was about business or farming, energy or technology, one matter kept rising to the top: waste management.

More than 60 percent of the countries submitting reports in preparation for the Earth Summit named solid waste disposal as their greatest environmental concern. At the conference, waste was cited as a cause of many of the environmental problems and a result of others. In some of the poorer countries, the delegates said, improper treatment of waste was responsible for one-third of all deaths. Clearly, if the environment was to be sustained, the problem of what to do with waste would have to be addressed.

There are basically only three things to do with waste: heap or bury it in landfills, burn it in the open or in incinerators, or recover it through reuse or recycling. The convention's delegates recognized that active measures to control waste were "of paramount importance for proper health, environmental protection … and sustainable development." What active measures did the delegates endorse? Chapter 4, section 19 of Agenda 21 gives their approach to the problem of waste:

> Society needs to develop effective ways of dealing with the problem of disposing of mounting levels of waste products and materials. Governments, together with industry, households and the public, should make a concerted effort to reduce the generation of wastes and waste products by:

a. Encouraging recycling in industrial processes and at the consumed level;

b. Reducing wasteful packaging of products;

c. Encouraging the introduction of more environmentally sound products.

Agenda 21 outlined a plan for waste management that incorporated the three Rs: reduce, reuse, and recycle. Each country was expected to come up with its own method of implementing the three Rs.

Toward a Solution

At that time, the United States—indeed, the entire world—was awash in waste. The volume of castoffs produced in America was 4.74 pounds (2.1 kg) per person per day. That amounted to a whopping 243.5 million tons (220.9 million metric tons) of trash in just one year! The amount was steadily rising. To meet Agenda 21 targets, leaders would not only have to figure out how to generate less trash; they would also have to come up with ways to reduce the mountains of waste already piled in landfills. That meant beginning with the third R: recycle.

Even before the Earth Summit, Americans were well aware of the problem of too much waste. They had stared at it on their television screens for

fact!

The United States has less than 5 percent of the world's population and produces at least 40 percent of the world's waste.

five months in 1987. The image was of the barge *Mobro 4000* in the waters of the Atlantic Ocean. It was loaded with more than 3,000 tons (2,722 metric tons) of garbage from New York City. Because New York City was running out of places to put its trash, the refuse was being hauled to North Carolina. When a rumor began that the garbage might contain toxic medical waste, North Carolinians refused to accept it. The *Mobro* went farther south, but its load was rejected by five more states and three foreign countries. The barge was forced to return to Long Island, where its cargo was burned and the ashes buried. The incident left the impression that the United States was running out of places to put its trash. It convinced Americans to get serious about recycling.

Serious Business

Getting serious about recycling meant stepping up the efforts already in place. When the *Mobro* was searching for a place to offload its garbage, only 1,050 cities in the United States offered curbside recycling. Most of the programs were voluntary. Four years later, at the close of the Earth Summit, the number of cities operating curbside recycling programs had quintupled, to 5,404. By 2006, the figure was 8,660.

In the early years of household recycling, people separated the recyclable items. Paper went into one bin, often having to be tied into bundles. Glass, cans, and plastics went into another bin. This is called dual-stream recycling. A **waste stream** is a flow of waste materials from their source to their final destination. For example, a medical waste stream contains items discarded from a hospital, and an industrial waste stream has the leftovers from factories. Dual-stream recycling means two streams of household waste materials. One stream, with newspapers, cardboard boxes, and other paper products, goes to paper processing plants. All

The Canadian Internationalist

Maurice Strong was uniquely positioned to lead international discussions of development and environment. He knew about development. From the age of nineteen, he led or helped lead a number of oil and gas companies and water and mineral resources businesses. He built a small, struggling, Canadian petroleum company into one of the biggest corporations in the energy industry. At the request of the prime minister, he steered Petro-Canada through the oil crisis of the 1970s. He was an entrepreneur, a financier, and a businessman; he knew economic development.

Strong also knew how economic development affected the environment. His work gave him a front-row seat to the damage that unwise development projects could bring to the land they exploited.

Strong also had experience in international relations. As a young man, his work took him to far northeastern Canada, where he lived among the Inuit people. Later, he installed service stations for an oil company in Kenya and traveled throughout Africa and Asia. As a volunteer with the YMCA, he chaired the committee that coordinated the international organization's chapters in different countries. Serving on the boards of several corporations, he had many opportunities to speak to international audiences of influential people.

Because of his knowledge and experience, Strong was asked to head the Canadian International Development Agency. In that role, he championed environmental causes, warning that economic development must be balanced with environmental conservation. He also served as one of his country's delegates to the United Nations.

When the UN planned the Conference on the Human Environment in Stockholm, Sweden, in 1972, the organizers asked Strong to lead it. The Stockholm conference, the first major intergovernmental convention on environmental issues, was a landmark event. It put concerns about the health of the planet front and center on the international stage, garnered the support and cooperation of nations previously hesitant to work together, and established Maurice Strong as the leading voice for global environmentalism. The Stockholm conference set the wheels in motion for the next big event, the Earth Summit in Rio, which would also be led by the Canadian oilman.

After the conferences, Strong continued to advocate for UN environmental programs. His tough stances on controversial issues such as environmental equality, greenhouse gas emissions, climate change, and world government earned him admiration from some people and condemnation from others. However history judges him, he will always be regarded as the father of the global environmental movement.

While the garbage-laden *Mobro* sat for five months off New York City,
Greenpeace activists climbed aboard to deliver a message.

other recyclable items go to a **materials recovery facility**, a giant building where they are sorted, processed, and sent to factories that use them to make new glass, metal, and plastic products.

In the 1990s, many cities switched to single-stream recycling, in which everything thought to be recyclable went into one big box. There were two reasons for the change. Environmentalists hoped that making recycling simpler would encourage people to become more serious about recycling. It did; more people participated, and they put more items in the recycling bins. At the same time, going from two streams to one cut collection time and costs in half.

Advances in technology made single-stream recycling possible. The commingled materials are dumped onto conveyer belts. After some hand sorting, a spinning device separates light and heavy items. Powerful magnets pull and push tin and aluminum in different directions. Sensors, air jets, optical scanners, and other high-tech equipment sort different types of paper, glass, and plastics.

The modern technology and the growing interest in preserving the environment have made recycling one of the biggest businesses in the United States. The recycling industry processes $90 billion of scrapped material a year. The material comes from several sources. Household waste is just one recycling stream. Other streams include automobiles, ships, debris from buildings and construction sites, appliances, and electronics. Workers in materials recovery facilities shred or crush the discarded items, extract whatever value is in them, and create **feedstock**, or raw material for manufacturers to use to produce new products.

Toward Zero Waste

However, every item put in a recycling bin is not completely recyclable. When all the value has been taken out, some material is often left over. What happens to the waste that remains after recycled items are converted to manufacturing feedstock? It gets sent to landfills. Despite great strides in recycling in the early twenty-first century, landfills continued to grow.

Landfills are not simply unsightly scars on the landscape; they are dangerous places. The major problems with old landfills have been fixed. The newer sites are lined so toxic matter does not seep into the ground and the groundwater. Modern incinerators burn some of the trash in ways that capture and store energy. However, as long as **organic waste** goes in landfills, landfills will continue to do harm to the environment.

Organic waste is material that is originally from a plant or an animal. Yard debris such as leaves and grass clippings, food scraps, and some paper products are organic waste. Organic materials are **biodegradable**; that is, they decompose, or break down, naturally. But when they are buried and therefore deprived of oxygen, they release methane gas as they decompose. Methane gas absorbs and traps the sun's heat, much like a greenhouse does. It is not the most common greenhouse gas, but it is one of the most potent. It has been linked to global warming and climate change.

One way the United States and other countries have attempted to keep from adding to their landfills is to ship their excess recyclables to other countries. Some countries, such as China, have a shortage of raw materials and an abundance of cheap labor. In those countries, buying recyclables and processing them into feedstock is the least expensive way to operate.

Exporting waste that would otherwise go in a landfill to a nation that might recycle it reduces waste, but it doesn't eliminate it. The goal of Agenda 21 is zero waste. The best way to get to zero waste is to cut it down at the source—the first R of the waste management hierarchy: reduce the amount of waste created.

Shifting the Burden

Reducing waste at the source means shifting the responsibility from the consumer, the person who uses a product, to the manufacturer, the company that makes the product. The first attempt to place the burden of reducing waste on manufacturers came in Germany in 1991.

At that time, Germany was running out of places to put its trash. The most common item clogging its landfills was packaging. Throwaway bottles, boxes, and other wrappings made up at least half of all household trash. The incinerators could not keep up with the 15.3 million tons (13.9 million metric tons) of packaging discarded every year. To reduce the waste, German leaders passed the Packaging Ordinance. This law required every company that used any kind of packaging to take the packaging materials back from consumers of their products free of charge and recycle or dispose of it.

fact!

Packaging constitutes about 65 percent of household trash and about one-third of most landfills.

To implement the law, a private company was formed to collect all the packaging: Duales System Deutschland (DSD). The manufacturers of products that use packaging fulfill their responsibility for taking back the packaging by paying DSD to collect and dispose of it for them. DSD charges the manufacturers a fee based on what materials they use in their packaging, how much the materials weigh, and how much of the materials they use. The fee structure encourages the manufacturers to use less packaging and less material in the packaging.

Manufacturers that use DSD receive a license to put a special logo on their products, called the Green Dot. The Green Dot

Egypt's Zabaleen

A small town on the edge of Cairo, Egypt's capital and largest city, is home to the Zabaleen. The name means "garbage people." The seventy thousand people of the little community make a living collecting the trash of Cairo. They have been doing it for seventy years.

The collection system is organized and efficient. The Zabaleen have divided the city and assigned sections to different families or groups. No one tries to work in someone else's area. There is no need to do so because there is plenty of garbage; the eighteen million people of Cairo generate 15,000 tons (13,608 metric tons) of trash a day. The people go door to door, most with donkey-drawn carts, charging the city's residents a small fee to carry away their rubbish.

The Zabaleen take the garbage to their town, where it sits in huge mounds. Entire families pick through and sort the refuse. The plastic bottles, aluminum cans, paper, and glass can be sold to factories. Other items can be remade into useful products that can also be sold. The Zabaleen boast a recycling rate of 85 percent, perhaps the highest of any city in the world. The food waste is fed to the town's pigs. The people live off the income from the sale of the trash, the collection fees, and the meat from their pigs. It is not a great living, but it is enough, and the Zabaleen are happy.

Or at least they were until 2004. That is when Egypt's president, Hosni Mubarak, grew tired of the donkey carts and decided to modernize the garbage collection. He hired three Western companies to take over the service. The companies placed bins on the city's streets, told the people to deposit their rubbish in the bins, and added a charge to their electric bills.

The professional waste management system did not work well. Residents who lived in high-rise buildings did not want to go down to the street to get rid of their trash. They had been used to the Zabaleen coming right to their door. The big companies recycled barely

In Zabaleen homes, people live on the upper floors; the ground floor is kept open for garbage sorting and recycling.

a quarter of what they collected, and they dumped much of the rest into the canals that ran through the city. The resulting pollution discouraged foreigners from coming to Cairo, and tourism suffered.

By 2013, the Egyptian leaders recognized the professional system was a failure. They invited the Zabaleen to organize into companies, gave them contracts, and supplied them with uniforms and official vehicles. The government accepted the Zabaleen as business people, and they are once again keeping the streets of Cairo clean.

German neighborhoods have at least seven different color-coded bins for sorting five types of trash and three kinds of glass.

is similar to the recycling symbol; it is a circle made of two interlocked arrows swirling together in a clockwise direction. Manufacturers that pay the collection and disposal fee can put the logo on all their products, even those without packaging. The Green Dot on an item does not mean the item is recyclable; it shows that the company that made the item participates in the DSD solution for manufacturer responsibility for reducing waste.

The German Success Story

Manufacturer responsibility is only half of Germany's solution to the waste problem; the other half is consumer responsibility. The law requires manufacturers to take back their packaging, but consumers have to get it to them. That is achieved through a uniform, nationwide system in which consumers separate their waste into color-coded bins. The bins are everywhere—at train stations, parks, schools, soccer stadiums, and other public places.

Homes and businesses also have the color-coded bins, and residents must put paper, packaging, food waste, and general garbage into the proper containers. Each bin has a bar code so users can be charged every time a bin is emptied. They pay by weight: a small fee for food scraps and recyclables, a large fee for garbage. The price difference helps people remember to recycle everything they can. Fines are levied if items are found in the wrong containers.

The system has been a phenomenal success. Recycling has become a habit in Germany; everyone does it. Germany recycles over 65 percent of its waste—more than any other country. The organic waste is turned into fertilizer or energy, the nonorganic into feedstock both for Germany and for sale to other nations. Everything that is not recycled is incinerated; none goes into a landfill. Modern technology enables incinerators to operate cleanly, capturing energy and converting it to electricity. In fact,

Germany has reduced its waste so much that it imports waste from Italy, Switzerland, and other countries so its incinerators can generate more energy.

Other nations in Europe have adopted the German model. Three years after Germany introduced the idea of producer responsibility for waste reduction, the European Union adopted a directive that extended the successful practices to all its members. As a result, twenty-eight countries, some outside the European Union, now use the Green Dot system.

Rethinking Recycling

Germany's success introduced a new element into the discussion of waste management: product design. When manufacturers had to pay for the recycling or disposal of their products' packaging, they started redesigning the packaging to produce less waste and thus reduce their disposal costs. Environmentally conscious manufacturers now try to design not just their packaging but also their products so the waste can be reduced, reused, or recycled. One way is to make the items completely or partially from recycled materials; this reduces waste. Another idea is to fashion a product for multiple uses, such as an infant car seat that converts to a booster chair for a toddler. This reuses what would otherwise be wasted.

A third option is to make the product with materials that are completely or nearly completely recyclable. This type of design is sometimes called "cradle to the grave." That means that through the entire life cycle of the product—from selection of raw materials (cradle), through the manufacturing process, through the use by the consumer, to the final disposal (grave)—care is taken to lessen the impact of the product on the environment. Some people call this zero waste.

But it is not really zero waste; the product still has an end, a grave. At the end of its useful life, there is usually some waste. Even products that are completely recycled produce waste, if only the wasted energy used in the collection, transportation, and recycling processes. Recycled products are often downcycled—that is, the recycled material, and thus whatever is made from it, is generally of lower quality than the original.

A different idea for product design was proposed by Michael Braungart and William McDonough in their 2002 book *Cradle to Cradle: Remaking the Way We Make Things*. They suggested that manufacturers attempt to upcycle, to design products that can be turned into something of equal or better quality at the end of their life cycle. Cradle-to-cradle design looks at waste not as something to be discarded or recycled, but as food for something better. The product would go from cradle (raw materials) to cradle (feedstock for a new product). This, the authors believed, is how nature really works.

Implementing the cradle-to-cradle concept is not easy, but it is not impossible. Both Nike and Puma have manufactured tennis shoes according to the cradle-to-cradle model. They are made of biodegradable materials. When they are no longer usable as shoes, they are shredded and completely broken down by microorganisms. The methane released in this process is captured, turned into energy, and used as fuel for the next product. Nothing is lost or wasted.

Cradle to cradle is not the same as recycling; it is a giant step beyond recycling. It replaces *recycle*—use as much of a product as possible again—with *return*—put all the resources that went into the product back into the economy. Cradle to cradle could completely rewrite the familiar waste management hierarchy; the new formula would be "Reduce, Reuse, Return."

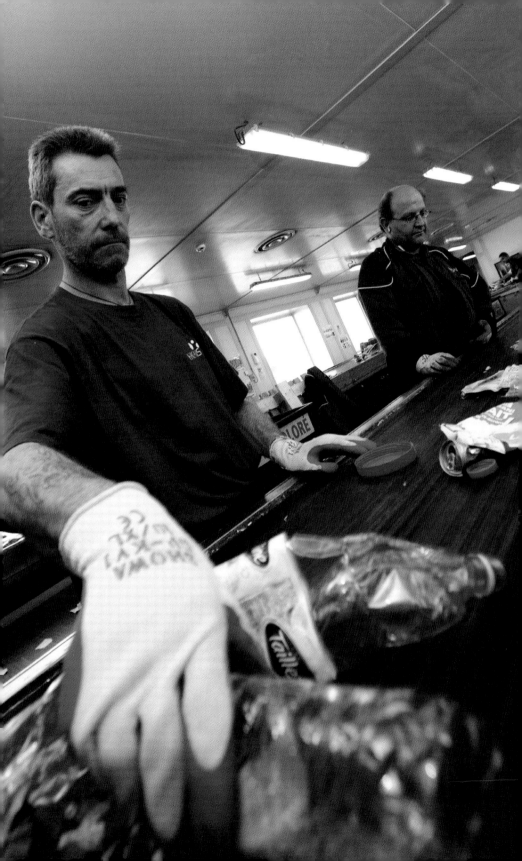

Everybody's Doing It … Or Are They?

Achieving zero waste takes the combined efforts of three parties: governments, manufacturers, and consumers. After the Earth Summit in Rio, from 1992 to 2012, the United Nations held three major conferences on the environment and development—in New York in 1997; in Johannesburg, South Africa, in 2002; and again in Rio in 2012. Between and after these mega conferences, scores of national and international summits continued to address issues of sustainable development. At least sixteen educational conferences focused on the environment in eight different countries just in June 2017. Governments around the world were determined to preserve the planet.

Manufacturers were also eager to promote sustainable development. Businesses and organizations put on workshops, conventions, exhibitions, and other events on environmental topics. They touted their work in preserving the environment

Opposite: A waste stream goes through multiple sortings. These men are separating plastics, aluminum, and paper on a conveyor belt.

and encouraged others to join them. Corporations wanted to do their part to create a clean world.

Many consumers committed themselves to cutting down on waste. Earth Day became an annual event that is now observed in nearly two hundred nations. Scout troops, clubs, and school groups conducted recycling drives. Organizations sprang up that focused on conservation, clean water, and eliminating pollution. Everybody, from government leaders to heads of corporations to private citizens, was aware of the many benefits of recycling.

Does It Really Matter?

Recycling not only reduces pollution; it also preserves the environment by conserving forests, water, minerals, and other natural resources. Recycling 1 ton (0.9 metric tons) of paper saves seventeen trees, 380 gallons (1,438 L) of oil, 3 cubic yards (2.3 cubic meters) of landfill space, and 7,000 gallons (26,497 L) of water. A ton of recycled steel recovers 2,500 pounds (1,133 kg) of iron ore, 1,400 pounds (635 kg) of coal, and 120 pounds (54 kg) of limestone. Conserving and recovering resources such as oil and minerals is important because these are **nonrenewable resources**. That is, they do not replace themselves; they are in limited supply, and once they are used up, they are gone. Forests are renewable, but most trees take years to grow to maturity, and we are using them up more quickly than we are replacing them. The World Wildlife Foundation estimates that Earth is losing 46,000 to 58,000 square miles (119,000 to 150,000 sq km) of forest every year, an area equal to losing forty-eight football fields per minute.

Recycling uses less energy than manufacturing something from raw materials. Making steel from recycled scrap takes 60 percent less energy than making it from iron ore; using recycled aluminum to make cans saves 90 percent of the energy it would take to produce them from scratch. Saving energy matters to the sustainability of the environment because energy consumes coal and oil, which are nonrenewable resources.

Another reason recycling matters is that it reduces the emission of greenhouse gases. The three most common gases that hold the sun's warmth in the atmosphere are carbon dioxide, nitrous oxide, and methane. The first two are released when waste is incinerated, the third when it is dumped into a landfill. Since methane is twenty-one times more potent than carbon dioxide as a heat-trapping gas, incinerating does less damage than landfill, but both are damaging. Recycling keeps some of the waste out of incinerators and landfills; thus it reduces global warming. Recycling matters to the sustainability of the planet.

Recycling is also good for the economy. It saves manufacturers money; producing goods from recycled feedstock is often cheaper than making them from raw materials. Recycling creates jobs: in the United States, 138,000 people are employed in the recycling industry. They work in waste management companies, scrap yards, materials recovery facilities, processing plants, and factories. Recycling creates more jobs than other forms of waste collection. According to the EPA, for every 10,000 tons (9,072 metric tons) of waste, incinerating creates one job, landfilling creates six jobs, and recycling creates thirty-six jobs. Recycling matters to our country's economic well-being.

How Are We Doing?

If recycling is so important to our planet and our economy, how seriously are we taking it? What progress have we made since the first Earth Summit issued a call to action over twenty-five years ago? Surprisingly, not very much. In 2000, the United States recycled almost 26 percent of all its waste. In 2013, that figure had climbed only slightly, to 35 percent. In 2000, Canadians recycled 19 percent of their waste; by 2013 they were recycling just a bit more, 24 percent.

Compare those figures with 2013 recycling rates in Europe. According to the Organization for Economic Co-operation and Development, six countries had rates in the forties, six had rates in the fifties, and Germany was at 65 percent. Why is Europe doing so much better than the United States and Canada?

One reason may be that the governments of many European countries have mandated some version of the German colored-bin system. That system requires people to sort their household waste. In the United States and Canada, most communities have opted instead for single-stream recycling. When cities switched from separating recyclables to single-stream collection in the 1990s, more people recycled and more materials were collected, but the amount of usable materials collected actually dropped. Mingling recyclables contaminates them. Paper gets wet; glass breaks into unrecoverable fragments and taints other items. The volume may be high, but the quality is low. About one-quarter of the items that could be recycled that come to materials recovery facilities through single-stream collection are not recycled; they end up in landfills.

A second reason Europe is ahead of North America in recycling is economic. European countries have financial incentives that encourage recycling for all three parties that play a role in working toward zero waste: governments, manufacturers, and consumers. For municipal governments, there are steep taxes and fines for placing anything in a landfill. For consumers, high collection fees for unrecyclable waste and low or no fees for recyclables promote recycling. Laws that require deposits on glass and plastic bottles encourage consumers to return them.

Perhaps the biggest economic incentive for recycling is producer responsibility legislation. Most European countries have enacted laws that make manufacturers responsible for disposal of their products at the end of their useful lives. This legislation has caused manufacturers to consider the entire life cycle of their products. They now design many items so they are more easily recyclable; they want to avoid the high landfill and incineration taxes.

In Europe, producer responsibility laws are nationwide. Although the United States has not established a similar national policy, at least thirty states have enacted laws that require manufacturers to pay for the cost of recycling or otherwise disposing of their products when consumers are finished with them. These laws, which are different in each state, apply to specific products, such as appliances, paint, mattresses, and carpets.

Confusing Plastics

One of the most common throwaway items is perhaps the most difficult to recycle: plastic. Plastic is inexpensive and durable, so it seems to be everywhere and in everything. More than 100 billion tons (90.7 billion metric tons) of plastic are manufactured worldwide every year. But plastic is particularly harmful to the environment for two reasons. First, it is made with oil, which is a nonrenewable resource. Second, most plastics are not biodegradable; they remain in landfills for hundreds of years. Therefore, reusing or recycling plastics is very important. However, people are often confused about what plastics can be recycled, and for good reason.

Plastics come in several forms. Some of the more common plastics are polystyrene (Styrofoam), PVC, PET, and HDPE and LDPE. PVC, or polyvinyl chloride, is used in squeeze

Lexington County landfill area before...

Lexington County landfill area after

A South Carolina county converted one of three landfills into a golf driving range and practice course. Here are before and after images.

bottles, flooring, loose-leaf binders, and many other items. PET, sometimes called PETE, is the abbreviated form of polyethylene terephthalate. It is the material in water bottles and some other food containers. HDPE and LDPE stand for high- and low-density polyethylene. These plastics are also made into many different items, the most familiar of which is probably the grocery bag. Plastics are everywhere—in milk cartons, clothes hangers, furniture, toys, wire insulation, and credit cards. Are they all recyclable?

The plastics industry devised a system that helps consumers distinguish the different types. The system assigns each kind of plastic a **resin identification code**. The code is a number, from one to seven, that specifies the resin from which the particular plastic is made. The number is stamped or printed directly on the object. Use of the code is voluntary, but many plastics carry it.

Originally the code appeared inside the three chasing arrows of the universal recycling symbol. But the code does not guarantee that a particular item can be recycled. In fact, municipalities have different standards for what they will accept in recycling bins. Most, but not all, curbside collectors will pick up PET, HDPE, and PVC plastics (numbers 1, 2, and 3). Few will accept any other plastics. To clear up the confusion for consumers, the chasing arrows around the resin identification codes were replaced with a simple triangle in 2013. Today, the only way for people to know what is recyclable in their area is to contact their local recycling collector.

One of the more controversial plastic items is the LDPE grocery bag. Not only can grocery bags be reused, but they are 100 percent recyclable. Recycled grocery bags can become new bags and other packaging; sturdy kitchen utensils; plastic lumber for fences, paneling, and outdoor decks; and a variety of other items. But very few are actually recycled. The problem is that even though they are recyclable, they cannot be processed along

fact!

with other plastics. The thin bags get stuck in the machinery at materials recovery facilities. Therefore, curbside collectors do not accept grocery bags, and they end up clogging landfills and littering oceans, streets, and neighborhoods.

What is the solution? Some grocery stores offer bag recycling. They have receptacles in which consumers can deposit their used carry-home bags, produce bags, bread wrappers, and other thin packaging. These are then taken to facilities that process the filmy materials separately from other plastics.

Some cities have tried to discourage consumers from using the bags by charging for them. Like the grocery store collection, this solution has met with limited success. San Francisco attempted to eliminate the problem altogether. In 2007, it became the first city in the country to ban certain categories of plastic bags. Other cities adopted the policy, and in 2016, California enacted a statewide ban on thin plastic bags in grocery stores, pharmacies, and convenience stores. Although people in some states vehemently object to the idea of such a ban, other states are considering following California's example.

Recycling Electronics

As ever-present as plastic bags seem to be, they are not the biggest challenge for recycling today. In both Europe and North America, e-waste—discarded electric appliances and electronic devices— makes up the fastest-growing waste stream. Every year, Americans purchase billions of consumer electronics, such as computers, televisions, game consoles, tablets, and cell phones, and every year they get rid of billions of these devices. According to the EPA, only 19 to 27 percent of e-waste is recycled, and most of that is larger items, such as refrigerators and televisions. Just 11 percent of mobile devices are recycled. Blame for the low e-waste recycling rate falls on all three parties with waste management responsibility: manufacturers, consumers, and government.

Electronics manufacturers encourage waste. They constantly make new products, and their practices persuade customers to buy the upgraded ones. The programs and accessories of the old devices do not work in the newer models. Producers often cancel support services for older products. Prices for repair or replacement parts are sometimes higher than for a brand-new item. These practices are called planned obsolescence because the makers purposely phase out the old, making it obsolete, when they bring in the new.

Consumers contribute directly to the mountains of waste. Everyone wants the latest features on their phones and the fastest speed on their laptops. The average length of time a person keeps an electronic device is two or three years. Printers, phones, and other electronics are often discarded long before their useful life has ended. Small devices that are considered either out of date or out of fashion are seldom taken to recycling centers; they are more often simply tossed into the trash.

Governments also share in the responsibility for the e-waste. The US Department of Energy standards for appliances and equipment have made manufacturers build their products with thinner materials and more electronics. Today's appliances are more energy efficient, but they do not last as long. Thus, more washers, dryers, and refrigerators are thrown away. Yet, the federal government does not impose any obligation on manufacturers to dispose of the broken or unwanted items. However, in the absence of national regulations, twenty-five states have some form of mandated producer take-back.

To fulfill their mandate, the manufacturers in those states contract with e-waste recyclers. These businesses have sprung up because there is value in discarded appliances and electronics. In addition to recyclable plastic, steel, and glass, some contain gold, copper, silver, and other metals, raw materials with many uses. The e-waste recycling companies extract and sell the value commodities, making a profit.

However, recycling electrical appliances and electronic devices is an expensive process. The items contain hazardous materials such as lead and mercury. Before magnets and other machinery can sort out the items with resell value, the devices must be disassembled by hand to remove the toxic components. That is a time-consuming step and is therefore costly. In the last several years, the prices for the recovered metals, steel, and plastic have dropped, so recycling companies do not make as much profit as they once did.

That means the most cost-effective way to handle the growing number of unwanted computers, tablets, and cell phones is to go to the second R of the waste management hierarchy. Many of the products can be repaired, refurbished, and reused. There are markets in North America and around the world for secondhand electronics among people who cannot afford the latest devices. Reuse is always the preferred method of dealing with castoffs.

Climbing the Ladder: The Reuse Movement

Reuse is better than recycling because it extends the life of an item. The longer an item remains in use, the fewer the number of new items needed to replace it. Making fewer items means using

The United Nations reported that about half the material in the e-waste sent to this dump in Agbogbloshie, Ghana, is recovered.

fewer resources and generating less waste. That is why Reuse is higher on the waste management hierarchy than Recycle.

Yet people recycle more than they reuse. Why? One reason is that most people are not aware of the importance or value of reuse. Another is that reusing is even less convenient than recycling. There is no curbside pickup for reusable items.

However, people concerned with sustainable development understand the need to look beyond recycling. Recycling has helped conserve renewable resources, lower greenhouse gas emissions, reduce the size of landfills, and create jobs. But recycling alone has only done so much. Landfills remain, resources are still being drained, and greenhouse gases are still being released. A new movement has begun to address this need: a reuse movement.

One of the first people to turn attention from recycling to reusing was Ira Baseman. An entrepreneur with a thrift store business, Baseman understood the life cycle of his products, primarily clothing, shoes, and accessories such as belts and purses. He knew the stats: 95 percent of clothing is reusable or recyclable, yet 85 percent is sent instead to landfills. He also knew that even if people in his Philadelphia neighborhood had more clothes than they cared to keep, there were people in other places, both in the United States and around the world, who did not. Baseman sold his thrift store and, in 2001, established a new business to keep the discarded apparel out of landfills and get it to people who could use it.

Although he called the company Community Recycling, it is really about reuse. He started raising awareness about reuse, not with consumers but with retailers, the people who sold the items when they were new. He convinced a few store owners to encourage their customers to come into the store and discard their old items when they bought new ones. Baseman then sold the boxes of used goods to organizations that distributed them to people who were grateful to have them. Over the years, the number of participating retailers has grown.

When the boxes reach places like Pakistan, Honduras, or Chile, they are often purchased by people who use the materials to stock small, family-owned thrift shops. These enterprising families resell the items at low prices their customers can afford. Reusing the items has accomplished far more than keeping materials out of landfills. It has enabled low-income people to obtain much needed clothing. It has helped people start businesses and has made local economies grow. It has created jobs both at home and abroad. And all of this has been at a profit for Community Recycling; it is a small-scale example of sustainable development.

The Movement Grows

Baseman started small, with just a few retailers. Before long, he expanded his collection outreach beyond stores to schools, organizations, and individuals. Today his company partners with more than five thousand organizations throughout the United States and in more than fifty other countries. It reuses over 1 million pounds (454,000 kg) of clothing every week.

Some might attribute the success of Community Recycling to the fact that it has made participation easy. When people fill boxes,

Implementing the Second R

Despite its name, the Electronic Recycling Association (ERA) does not recycle electronics. The mission of the Canadian nonprofit organization, according to its website, is "to reduce electronic waste and the negative impact it has on our environment, and to reuse unwanted computers and related electronic equipment through recovery, refurbishment and computer donation programs." The organization's focus is on "reuse," the second R of the waste-management hierarchy. ERA collects discarded hardware, removes the original user's data, gets it working well, and donates it to a charity. If something cannot be reused, ERA sends it to another organization for recycling.

ERA's founder and president, Bojan Paduh, knows the value of a computer, even an old one. He immigrated to Canada from Croatia in 1996, a young man with very few possessions. Someone in his new country gave him a computer, which, he said, had an "immeasurable impact" on his life. It led him to pursue a career in computer science.

Paduh was surprised to learn that heaps of computers sat in landfills, most still functioning. He began collecting them as a hobby, rebuilding them, and giving them to people in need, as someone had once done for him. His knowledge of technology and its importance in modern society, his concern for people who had no access to that technology, and his desire for better

A technician at an electronics recycling facility uses both high-tech and low-tech equipment to dismantle an unwanted desktop computer.

management of e-waste culminated in the establishment of the Electronic Recycling Association in 2004.

In addition to donating computers, ERA regularly holds Parts to PC workshops for twelve- to fifteen-year-olds. In the free two-hour sessions, the youths dismantle and reassemble a computer, learning its basic components and how it works. ERA also has a Moolah for Macros program that helps groups collect unused electronics to raise money for the donated computers for themselves or a charity of their choice.

ERA was founded on the idea that destroying something that still has use is unnecessary, wasteful, and irresponsible. The most responsible way to treat unneeded electronics, both environmentally and socially, is to reuse them. ERA's technicians evaluate the items they receive to estimate how much life is left before they refurbish them. They use parts from nonworking computers to rebuild others. When any item has no life at all, then and only then is it ready for recycling.

This couple makes and sells lamps from recycled materials. They collect pipes, glass, and other materials at flea markets and garage sales.

they simply go to the company's website, print a shipping label, and send the cartons off at no charge. But the real reason for the company's success is not convenience. It is attitude toward reuse.

When Baseman began his reuse project, he incorporated an idea reminiscent of the early environmental movements. The people leading those movements had a personal, emotional connection with what they were doing. They had seen news footage of environmental disasters, and some had been directly involved, cleaning the feathers of oil-soaked birds off Santa Barbara or protesting companies that spewed pollutants into the air of their cities. People in the early movements looked at recycling not as an economic or social good, but as a cause they cared about. Baseman infused that same personal connection into the reuse movement.

When someone turns a box of gently used items over to Baseman for reuse, that act is not the last the donor hears of the box. For every object Baseman handles, he keeps records of where the materials came from, where they go, and what happens to them when they get there. He shares this information with the donor, engaging the donor in the entire experience. People can put notes in the boxes if they choose. Baseman wants the individuals supplying the articles not to think in terms of things, but of people. He views the reuse movement as people helping other people improve their lives.

Green Industries: Using All Three Rs

Reuse is just one part of sustainable development. Companies that are serious about sustainable development incorporate all three Rs of the waste management hierarchy in their operations. To protect the environment and sustain its resources, reduction is always the first strategy. When reduction is not possible, reuse is the next option, followed by recycling. Businesses that follow this pattern and adopt other sustainable practices are called green businesses.

One industry with a number of green businesses is the construction trade. Green builders pay attention to all three Rs in the materials they choose and the ways they use energy and water. First, they reduce waste wherever possible. Green builders plan their projects to avoid unnecessary use of energy and water in the finished product. They orient buildings and place windows in positions that take maximum advantage of the sun's rays; this reduces the amount of energy required to heat and light the finished building. They place trees strategically so their shade reduces the need for energy to cool the building. In climates with little rainfall, green builders plant drought-resistant vegetation, reducing water waste.

Green builders reduce waste by using recycled materials whenever possible. They install roof shingles made from old tires, bottlestone countertops reconstructed from broken glass, and sidewalks and driveways made of concrete from demolished streets and highways. The really serious green builders do all their paperwork on recycled paper!

Where the materials come from is also important to waste reduction. Transporting products by truck uses diesel fuel, a nonrenewable resource that needs to be conserved. Green builders try to use materials produced within 500 miles (805 km) of the construction site to cut down on diesel fuel usage.

When waste reduction is not practical, green builders go to the second R, reuse. Items for reuse come from demolition of properties. Many items can be salvaged from buildings slated for destruction by careful dismantling, such as cabinets, doors, plumbing fixtures, bricks, and hardware. These items are frequently sold to contractors and the public at relatively low prices. Not only does this reuse reduce waste (sustainability), it also puts what would otherwise be wasted back into the economy (development).

What cannot be reused is recycled whenever possible. Lumber, pipes, and wire not needed at one location can be used at another. Builders take leftover items to warehouses or list them on exchanges so other builders can purchase them at discounted rates. Construction debris is taken to facilities that specialize in recycling building materials.

Recycling is also used to reduce water waste. Water may appear to be plentiful, and it is technically a renewable resource. However, Earth's supply of drinkable water is actually shrinking, so conserving water is important. Green builders design structures that capture rainwater and store it for watering lawns. They make driveways and sidewalks that allow water to trickle through, replenishing the water in the ground. They install systems that filter and treat wastewater from washing machines and sinks, recycling it for use in the buildings' plumbing.

Dealing with waste is only one part of sustainable development. To preserve resources for future generations, businesses must also think about the raw materials and the processes they use. But no matter how renewable the resources and how clean and energy efficient the processes, waste will always be an issue. Therefore, reduction, reuse, and recycling are of utmost importance in leaving a healthy and prosperous world to those who come after us.

4

Balancing Acts

Sustainable development, the catchphrase of the modern environmental movement, is a matter of balance. The twin goals of environmental preservation (sustainability) and economic gain (development) have to be pursued together. One cannot come at the expense of the other. Recycling, one element of the movement, is also a matter of balance between competing interests. Those interests include the general public, the recycling industry, and consumers of the recyclables and the recycled products.

People sometimes think of recycling as a benevolent practice, something good the general public does for the environment. Although that is true, recycling is a for-profit enterprise. The companies that collect the bins, the people who run the sorting facilities, and the plants that manufacture goods with recycled feedstock are all in business to make money. Recycling works only because it is a profit-making business.

Opposite: Three wind turbines between the two towers of the World Trade Center in Bahrain generate electricity for the fifty-story building.

Today, the recycling industry faces a number of challenges to its ability to make a profit. Those challenges involve changes in the way people recycle, changes in the way the industry processes the recycled items, and changes in the demand for recycled materials.

Balancing Supply with Changing Demand

For three decades, until 2010, recycling was a good business. After Earth Day 1990, the number of people recycling, the number of processing centers, and the number of jobs in the industry rose year by year. The growth enabled materials recovery facilities to develop new technologies to handle even more items at lower costs. Recycling companies had, literally, tons of materials.

In every business, profitability is determined by supply and demand. Environmentally conscious citizens gave the processing companies plenty of supply. Economic conditions created a great demand. Manufacturers of many products found that recycled feedstock was cheaper than **virgin material**, or raw resources such as iron ore, petroleum, and aluminum. The recycled products worked just as well. Purchasing from recyclers lowered the manufacturers' production costs.

Recyclers also discovered a demand overseas. In the 1990s and early 2000s, places like China, India, Russia, South Africa, and Brazil were growing their economies at a fast pace. These countries had a strong labor force but not enough raw resources to support manufacturing. The developed nations of North America and Europe were making waste these countries could turn into consumer goods. One region's waste became another region's resources.

Because of the demand, especially in the developing countries, the recyclables commanded a good price both at home and on the international market. But markets fluctuate. Price swings were particularly wide for oil, which is the base from which plastics are made. At the end of 1998, the price of oil plunged to an all-time low. It came up somewhat, but it fell again in 2009 and 2016. When oil is cheap, making plastic items from oil is less expensive than producing them from discards. Demand for recyclable plastics, and thus the price recyclers could charge for them, dropped steeply with the decline in oil prices.

Similar market changes affected other recyclables. Global demand for metal was particularly high in the 1990s, when India, China, and other countries were in a building frenzy. Short of their own supplies, they imported scrap metal. Recycling companies made huge profits. They reinvested the profits into new equipment so they could process and sell even more scrap. They installed huge crushers to flatten aluminum, baling machines to package the materials quickly, and giant scales that could weigh massive containers of the metals. But the building boom came to an end, and countries stopped buying so much scrap. Prices for scrap metal plummeted, and recyclers were left with excess materials and bills for the equipment they had bought on credit.

The market for used paper, the biggest waste commodity market, suffered as well. The largest purchaser of America's used paper was (and still is) China. With very few forests, Chinese papermakers manufactured poor quality products from grass, straw, and reeds. When the country began to industrialize rapidly, manufacturers imported millions of tons of scrap paper and reprocessed it, making paper and cardboard. But China's growth and its economy slowed, and worldwide demand for waste paper dropped. The price of waste paper on the global market in 2015 was less than half of what it was in 2010.

General economic stagnation also contributed to depressed sales and lower prices of recyclables. Prices of many products,

Paper recycled into packaging material in Hong Kong is loaded onto barges to be shipped elsewhere.

not just waste, fell after the economic downturn that began in 2008. Despite some grim statistics, recycling remains a profitable business, but the profits are not as high as they once were.

The Changing Supply

Decreased demand for recyclable waste is just one of the threats to recyclers' ability to make a profit. There are also challenges on the supply side of the supply-and-demand equation. The volume and the quality of the supply of recyclable waste are declining. The decline is a result of changes in manufacturing and in collection.

In the United States, the change in manufacturing began before the big drop in the price of oil. The price had skyrocketed in 1973 from $19.69 a barrel to $52.38. By 1970, it had more than doubled, to $119.25, with no end in sight. High oil prices meant huge increases to manufacturers in the cost of transporting their wares. Because fuel costs were determined by the weight of the load being carried, manufacturers began cutting down where they could on the weight of their products, making them thinner and lighter. For example, a single-serving plastic water bottle made today weighs about half of what it weighed ten years ago. A company can use the same amount of fuel today it used ten years ago and ship almost twice as many bottles.

The change was smart for manufacturers. They saved money twice, by using less material in the production and requiring less fuel for transportation, but the change was costly for recyclers. Now it takes more items to make the same volume. In 1972, twenty-two empty aluminum cans weighed 1 pound (16 ounces); today 1 pound consists of thirty-six cans. It takes one thousand more plastic bottles to make 1 ton of recycled plastic than it did in 1980. However, the number of citizens putting bottles and cans in recycling bins has not gone up. That means collectors must collect

A Fortune in Paper

In 2006, *Forbes Magazine* named Zhang Yin the richest woman in China. She began her ascent to that position twenty-one years earlier with $3,800. She was in the right place at the right time.

The right place was the city of Shenzhen, where Zhang worked as an accountant for a paper trading company. The job let her see how reusing waste paper improved the quality of her country's paper products. The right time was the 1980s, when China was just beginning to open its economy and permit private investment. It was also a time when supplies of raw materials could not keep up with China's racing economic development. Someone had told her that waste paper was like a forest; it could be recycled over and over. So Zhang moved to Hong Kong, then a British colony where conducting business was easier than in China proper, and used her life savings to begin a paper trading company.

That was in 1985. In 1990, frustrated with the shortage of waste paper available to her company and its poor quality, she moved to Los Angeles to personally negotiate purchases of better materials. In the United States, she founded a new company, America Chung Nam. The company collected used paper from American recyclers and shipped it to China.

Five years later, Zhang returned to Hong Kong to open a new business together with her husband and her brother.

Zhang Yen, or Yan Cheung, is active in several business and trade organizations. Here she is at an international conference in March 2017.

That business, Nine Dragons Paper, has become the largest manufacturer of paper packaging in Asia and one of the largest in the world. It has earned the billionaire recycler the nickname "Trash Queen."

In China, Nine Dragons Paper specializes in cardboard and containerboard, corrugated paperboard used for sturdy items such as boxes. It uses the waste paper supplied by Zhang's Los Angeles business. The two companies form a closed-loop operation: waste paper from America Chung Nam in the United States goes to Nine Dragons in China. It is made into boxes and sent back to the United States as packaging for many "made in China" products. In the United States it becomes waste paper, and the cycle begins all over again.

fact!

more and materials recovery facilities must sort and process more for every ton of usable recyclable waste. The additional work costs additional dollars; the recyclers lose money twice.

Curbside collection has also affected supply in ways that hurt recyclers financially. When single-stream collection was introduced, more recyclable items poured into the recovery facilities, but so did obviously unrecyclable articles such as dirty diapers, used syringes, and dead animals. Some of the materials people assumed were appropriate, such as the flimsy plastic wrapping for paper towels and the like, gummed up the machines of the processing plants. Commingling of different materials produced contamination that led to rejection of otherwise recyclable items. This also is a double loss; the processing facilities lose the money the rejected items should bring them, and they must pay to add the items to a landfill.

Balancing Costs and Benefits

If recycling companies cannot make decent profits, how long will they stay in business? The biggest recycler in the United States, Waste Management, Inc., shut down thirty of its facilities in just two years and is planning to close more. In California, more than 450 processing plants went out of business in 2016. These companies decided recycling was not worth the cost to them.

What about the rest of us? What about our country? Our planet? Are the benefits of recycling worth the costs? The greatest benefit is that recycling conserves natural resources and sustains the environment. The EPA lists several specific benefits, but some of them come with a cost:

- Recycling reduces the amount of waste in landfills; but it costs more to recycle most items than to put them in a landfill.

- By keeping material out of landfills, recycling reduces air and water pollution; but the recycling process creates toxic wastes that are sent to landfills.

- Recycling reduces greenhouse gas emissions; but materials recovery facilities use chemicals that release toxic pollutants.

- By reducing the need to extract raw materials, recycling saves energy; but the vehicles that collect recyclables and the processing plants expend energy.

Do the benefits outweigh the costs? The answer is actually different for different items. Paper, metals, and plastics are not the same in terms of how much it costs to recycle them. Nor are they the same in how much energy and resources are saved when they are recycled. Recycling steel saves 60 percent of the energy that would be used to make it from virgin material, but recycling an aluminum can saves 95 percent. The only way to know if recycling is worth the benefits is to evaluate each item or at least each category of material. Environmentalists and manufacturers do this through a process called life-cycle assessment.

At the 11-acre (4.5 ha) Sims Materials Recovery Center in New York, recycling begins with trucks unloading tons of municipal discards.

Life-cycle assessment is an analysis of a manufactured product that determines its effects on the environment. It examines the entire life cycle of the article, from cradle to grave. Every product goes through several stages throughout its life: getting the raw materials, making the product, getting the product to the consumer, using the product, and disposing of the product at the end of its use. The activities at each stage use energy and produce waste. A life-cycle inventory measures the inputs and outputs at each stage. The measurements are put into formulas that are used to calculate the impact of the product on the environment throughout its life cycle.

Producers use life-cycle assessment to make decisions about how they design and manufacture their products. They compare costs and benefits of various environmental impacts. For example, some of the components of an automobile could be made from either steel or plastic; which has the lesser effect on the environment? Looking at the "using the product" life stage, plastic is preferable because a heavier car (made of steel) would require more fuel for operation. But considering the "disposing at end of use" stage, steel wins because steel is recycled much more easily and more completely. Plugging actual numbers into the formulas tells the manufacturer how much energy is saved at each stage and therefore whether plastic or steel is the better energy saver for a particular car.

The Fourth R

Recycling is only one environmentally sustainable option for end-of-use disposal. Another possibility is to burn the unusable material, generating energy in the process. This is called waste to energy (WtE) or energy from waste (EfW). Because it reclaims some of the energy that went into making and using the products

Challenging Students

One of the challenges to recycling is a lack of awareness; people do not understand the importance of recycling, what can be recycled, and how to do it. The Recycling Council of Ontario, Canada, has been chipping away at that challenge. Its mission is to "inform and educate all members of society" so they can minimize their impact on the environment. The council takes advantage of Canada's annual Waste Reduction Week (the third week of October) to challenge children as well as adults to begin and maintain environmentally responsible habits.

One of its successful programs is the Waste-Free Lunch Challenge. Mindful of the statistic that the waste left over from just one student's school lunches amounts to 66 pounds (30 kg) a year, the council helps schools encourage elementary students to reduce that number. For one week, students bring their lunches in reusable lunchboxes, avoiding any throwaway wrappings. The food is packed in reusable containers, and any leftovers, such as banana peels or uneaten food, go home in the containers to be eaten later or composted. The school inventories students' lunches before and during the challenge and reports the results. Prizes are awarded to schools that show the greatest waste reduction.

For secondary students, the challenge is to "give a shirt." By the time they are in high school, Ontario's students are expected to already understand the importance of recycling. The Give a Shirt Challenge teaches them about reuse. Students bring gently used clothing, shoes, purses, backpacks, and similar articles to school during Waste Reduction Week. The items are collected at the schools and sent to organizations that reuse them locally and globally. The few items that cannot be reused are repurposed as upholstery, rags, or insulation.

Around Earth Day, the council issues a Grab Bag Challenge. To promote recycling, cash prizes are offered to students who collect the most plastic bags. Schools can win a bench made of 95 percent recycled materials, a permanent reminder of the value of recycling. In 2016, schoolchildren collected over two million bags during the challenge. The hope is that the students develop good attitudes and habits about the three Rs that will last a lifetime.

being disposed of, this option is called "recovery." Many countries and companies add recovery to the waste management hierarchy, just below recycle and just above burial in a landfill. It is sometimes thought of as the fourth R.

Recovery is not a new method of dealing with waste. There have always been only three ways to handle physical materials at the end of their lives: recycle, incinerate, or put in a landfill. WtE is incineration, but it uses the incineration to produce energy, usually in the form of electricity. In a WtE plant, waste materials are burned at temperatures as high as 2000 degrees Fahrenheit (1093 degrees Celsius). The heat is applied to water to make steam. The steam powers a turbine, and the turbine produces electricity. The electricity is used to heat or power homes and businesses in the area near the facility. For every ton of waste, enough energy is recovered to power a household for a full month.

About 10 percent of the waste fed into a WtE incinerator does not burn, but some of it is still usable. Magnets pull metals out of the unburned matter, and the metals are recycled. Most of the remaining ash is also recycled, used in roadbeds and embankments for railways. Thus no more than 5 percent of the original waste ends up in landfills.

The old methods of incineration were stopped because they released pollutants, toxic chemicals, and greenhouse gases into the atmosphere. The old systems were open, spilling everything into the air; today's WtE facilities use closed systems. Modern technology has enabled WtE operators to neutralize the toxins and contain the gases so they do not harm people or the environment.

Europe is ahead of North America in the use of the fourth R. In Belgium, Denmark, Sweden, Norway, and the Netherlands, practically all waste that is not reused or recycled is incinerated in WtE plants. These facilities are major suppliers of heat and

This WtE plant in Zurich, Switzerland, converts 110,000 tons (100,000 metric tons) of waste each year into heat for eight thousand households and electricity for thirteen thousand.

power in these countries, where fossil fuels such as coal are scarce. In fact, the nations have become so efficient in the four Rs, they have to purchase waste from their neighbors in order to generate all the heat and electricity they need. In 2014, Sweden imported 800,000 tons (725,748 metric tons) of trash.

Weighing Alternatives

Waste to energy appears to be a win-win, eliminating nonrecyclable waste and recovering energy. It has been celebrated as an alternative to landfills, especially in Europe, where there is no space for any more landfills. However, WtE is not without problems.

Perhaps the biggest concern is whether toxins and pollutants are truly controlled. Even in the closed systems, some harmful emissions seep into the air. The toxic gases may affect the workers in the plants, if no one else. The relatively small amount of pollutants that are emitted are trapped in filtered bags and deposited in special landfills designated for hazardous materials. But do those bags eventually leak? Does the ash that ends up in road construction contain any residual toxins? These questions raise another concern: the pollution control measures are expensive. The cost to build a WtE facility starts at $100 million, and half that price tag is for pollution control. After the initial investment, there are costs for operation, equipment

fact!

The average life of paper money is fewer than five years. In Philadelphia, San Francisco, and Los Angeles, old currency is burned in WtE facilities and powers homes and businesses.

maintenance, and monitoring of the special disposal sites. Critics believe these expenses, together with the environmental and health concerns, make landfilling a better solution.

Critics also dismiss the main argument for WtE, which is that it produces energy. Energy, they point out, is not really an issue. The United States has a limitless supply of renewable energy in the sun and wind. Many environmentalists say that what is really needed is more attention to the development of solar and other forms of energy.

The biggest criticism of waste to energy is that it discourages the activities that are higher on the waste management ladder. For the facilities to function properly, they must have high volumes of waste. People who depend on WtE for energy may be tempted to feed materials that could be reused or recycled into the incinerators. Manufacturers may rely on WtE to meet their obligation for end-of-life product disposal and therefore not try to design items with less waste.

Thus the fourth R is not an alternative to landfilling. It is an alternative to Reduce, Reuse, and Recycle. It might make good use of waste, but it cannot eliminate it. The original waste management hierarchy is still the key to the sustainable development of a beautiful world.

5

The Three Rs Today

S ince the first Earth Day in 1970, enthusiasm for protecting and preserving the environment has grown. The ecology movements progressed from outrage at pollution to recognition of the deeper and more complex need for sustainable development. With each new phase, consumers got a little better at recycling and manufacturers got a little better at reduction. Everyone learned new and better ways of implementing the three Rs.

Many of those new ways continue to be practiced today. Curbside pickup, single-stream recycling, and waste-to-energy recovery have become commonplace. The evolution of recycling also led to the creation of new products that are now part of our daily lives: durable plastic lumber, cellulose insulation, and packing peanuts, to name a few.

Innovation continues as society has risen to the challenge of making recycling, reuse, and recovery increasingly more efficient.

Opposite: At recycling facilities, recycled bottles are pressed into blocks, then ground into pieces. These chips will be made into thread.

Some organizations incorporate recycling into their activities. Collecting discarded plastic at public parks benefits the environment and helps the community.

For example, scientists are experimenting with a technology called pyrolysis. At high temperatures and without oxygen, tires and other discarded plastics can be converted to gas fuel. Other researchers are exploring ways to make rubber for tires and other products from renewable materials such as grass, corn, and trees.

Accepting Responsibility

One of the important ideas to come from the recycling movement is that manufacturers should bear responsibility for the waste their products leave behind. The concept, and in some cases the mandating, of producer responsibility keeps the three Rs at the forefront of nearly every industry. From the design of their products to the processes they use in making and distributing them, businesses consciously strive to reduce the amount of waste they create and make their products reusable or recyclable.

Companies today are working toward a goal of zero waste. They use terms like the "circular economy," "closed-loop recycling," and "cradle-to-cradle manufacturing" to describe how to achieve zero waste. The idea is to manufacture products that can be completely

fact!

Growth of Recycling in the United States

The figures below show the increases in percentage of total waste Americans recycled from 1960 to 2013.

Year	Percentage
1960	6.4
1965	6.2
1970	6.6
1975	7.3
1980	9.6
1985	10.1
1990	16.0
1995	25.7
2000	28.5
2005	31.4
2010	34.0
2013	34.3

Artist Bruce Munro built towers for England's Salisbury Cathedral from fifteen thousand recycled water bottles. Combined, the sixty-nine lighted towers use the same energy as four 60-watt bulbs.

recycled. If all the components of an item can be used to create a new item, the resources travel in a circle, closing any loops that would allow waste to seep out. The ultimate goal is that after many cycles in the circular economy, the resources are returned to the earth, the cradle from which they came. Manufacturers are rethinking everything they do, with the three Rs as their guide.

To put the three Rs into practice in their production processes, manufacturers need consumers to supply them with their discards. However, consumers' commitment to recycling has not always been strong. Some manufacturers that have redesigned their products so they are made from recyclable materials cannot get enough of those materials. Because businesses are taking their responsibility to environmental sustainability seriously, ten companies have stepped in to address this problem. In 2014, they joined together and came up with a plan to boost consumer recycling.

The companies were among the giants in several industries: 3M, Colgate-Palmolive, Coca-Cola, Goldman Sachs, Johnson and Johnson, Keurig Green Mountain, PepsiCo, Procter & Gamble, Unilever, and Walmart. They established the Closed Loop Fund to lend money to cities and businesses whose recycling programs were struggling. Each company contributed $5 million to $10 million. Municipalities can use the funds to improve collection; businesses can invest the money in equipment that increases the efficiency of their processing facilities.

The zero-interest (for municipalities) and low-interest (for private businesses) loans are kick-starting stagnant recycling programs. Some cities have purchased bins and carts and begun or upgraded curbside collection. Others have bought trucks and added new routes to their collection programs. The expansions are bringing more recyclable items into materials recovery facilities.

A Zero-Waste Company

Achieving zero waste does not seem possible, but one company came close. In 2013, the US Zero Waste Business Council awarded the Sierra Brewing Company its first-ever platinum certification for operations that were 99.8 percent waste-free. To achieve that level, the Chico, California, company reuses or recycles nearly everything. Scrap metal, shrink-wrap, even office paper is reused. When supplies like bottle caps arrive, the boxes are saved and used for outgoing shipments. The grains that are left over after use in the brewing process are fed to local cattle and dairy cows. All organic material that does not go to the cows is composted, enriching the fields where the company grows its grains. Growing its own hops and barley on site not only enables the business to use the compost; it also eliminates the need for fuel to transport the grains to the brewery.

The company does not waste fuel when it distributes its product. Deliveries are scheduled so that drivers can pick up supplies or whatever else they need after they drop off their orders. The company's trucks are never empty. They do not stop at gas stations; they run on biofuel made from oil from the company's restaurant.

The brewery employs a number of energy-saving strategies and devices: heat recovery systems on equipment, sensors on lights, and more than ten thousand solar panels. The brewery is a green building, equipped with many energy- and water-saving features. Sierra Brewing Company has certainly earned its platinum certification.

With their new equipment, the owners of the recovery facilities are able to process the materials more efficiently, giving manufacturers the feedstocks they need to close the loop as tightly as possible. Thus one of the legacies of the recycling movement has been corporations' encouragement and facilitation of consumer recycling.

Opportunities for Reuse

Municipalities, factories, and large corporations are not the only entities impacted by the recycling movements. The general public has remained conscious of the environmental, economic, and social values of the three Rs. Consumers have been doing more than dropping their castoffs into recycling bins. They have also been coming up with ideas for reusing and repurposing a variety of items. Nonprofit organizations are continually springing up with novel ways for average citizens to help preserve the environment while making a difference in people's lives. Check out some of these opportunities where you can be involved:

The Crayon Initiative recycles crayons from restaurants, schools, and individuals. The wax in crayons is not biodegradable, so crayons cannot be placed in home recycling bins. However,

fact!

Recycling Report Card

Many countries are working hard on improving their recycling to keep up with waste generation. Below are the changes from 2000 to 2013 in the amounts of municipal waste recycled and composted per person for some nations.

Germany	16%
Canada	21%
United States	25%
Denmark	54%
France	71%
United Kingdom	256%
Chile	–78%

the pieces can be combined and remade into like-new crayons. The group gives the recycled products to hospitals, where they provide entertainment, education, and therapy to children. You can gather crayons or organize collection drives and events at a school, club, or workplace.

Recycle-A-Bicycle is a program in New York City that teaches young people to refurbish old bicycles. The organization sells the bicycles and uses the profit for youth programs. Every year, the recycling operation salvages about 1,800 bicycles, keeping them out of landfills, and teaches job skills to one thousand youths. If you do not live in New York City, you might consider starting a similar program in your community. You could restore and repurpose cell phones or other electronics, stuffed animals, jewelry, furniture, or whatever items you know how to repair.

You don't need to have a lot of resources to begin a reuse adventure. In 2004, twelve- and thirteen-year-old siblings Robbie and Brittany Bergquist had only twenty-one dollars when they started a drive to collect and recycle cell phones. Their idea was to fix the phones, sell them, and donate the money they received to purchase calling cards and minutes of talk time for service men and women stationed overseas. That twenty-one dollars has grown into a national nonprofit that has given more than three hundred million minutes and over five million prepaid calling cards. In addition, it has kept more than fifteen million cell phones out of the waste stream.

These are just a few of the organizations that repurpose clothing, health-care equipment, baby strollers, art supplies, eyeglasses, sporting goods, pet supplies, and dozens more items. Reusing through nonprofits such as these has two benefits in addition to reducing waste. It allows you to move one rung up the waste management ladder and therefore closer to the goal of sustaining the environment through zero waste. And because

Here, a woman puts a cell phone into a collection box. Japan's Olympic Committee hopes to collect 8 tons (7.26 metric tons) of metal from donated cell phones for the 2020 Olympic and Paralympic medals.

many of these organizations give the donated articles to people who need them, contributing to these groups lets you play a part in someone's personal and economic development.

Implementing the three Rs today is about sustainable development. It is about the planet as well as the people who inhabit it. It is about both preserving the environment and making a difference in the lives of people.

Glossary

biodegradable Able to be decomposed into natural materials by microorganisms.

composting Incorporating organic waste into soil so it fertilizes and conditions the soil as it decays.

discard An item that is not used or wanted, or to dispose of an unused or unwanted item.

ecologist A person who studies the relationship between living things and their environment.

ecology The study of the relationships between living things and their environment. "Ecological" is sometimes used to mean the same thing as "environmental."

feedstock Raw material used to make new products.

greenhouse gas A gas that absorbs radiation from the sun and traps heat in the atmosphere, warming Earth like a greenhouse.

hierarchy An arrangement of objects or actions in order of importance.

landfill An area of ground built up, or filled in, with materials brought from somewhere else. Often the materials consist of trash and garbage covered with dirt.

materials recovery facility A building in which recyclable items are sorted and processed to collect any materials from the items useful in making new products.

nonrenewable resource A raw material, such as coal or natural gas, that does not regenerate itself.

organic waste Material that is originally from a plant or an animal, such as food scraps, agricultural waste, and grass and other yard debris.

resin identification code A number that appears on an item made of plastic that identifies the type of material from which the plastic is made.

salvage Rescue from being destroyed; items so rescued.

sustainable development Economic growth that uses resources to meet the needs of the present without using up resources that might be needed in the future.

virgin material Natural resources such as timber or metal ore that have not been treated or processed.

waste stream The flow of waste materials from their source to their final destination.

Further Information

Books

Barker, David M. *E-waste*. Ecological Disasters. Minneapolis, MN: Essential Library, 2017.

Perdew, Laura. *The Great Pacific Garbage Patch*. Ecological Disasters. Minneapolis, MN: Essential Library, 2017.

Scherer, Lauri S. *Recycling*. Issues That Concern You. Farmington Hills, MI: Greenhaven, 2014.

Thorsheim, Peter. *Waste into Weapons: Recycling in Britain During the Second World War*. Studies in Environment and History. New York: Cambridge University Press, 2016.

Websites

Earth Day Network
http://www.earthday.org
The blog on this website has interesting articles, and the site's pages offer a variety of specific ways people can take action to preserve the environment.

Zero Waste International Alliance
http://zwia.org
The website of the alliance has case studies and articles about zero-waste practices and progress, and links to international organizations and businesses pursuing zero waste.

Organizations

Greenpeace International
Ottho Heldringstraat 5
1066 AZ Amsterdam
The Netherlands
Tel: +31 20 718 2000
Email: info.int@greenpeace.org
http://www.greenpeace.org/international/en/about/worldwide

Institute of Scrap Recycling Industries
1250 H Street, NW, Suite 400
Washington, DC 20005
(202) 662-8500
Email: isri@isri.org
http://www.isri.org

Keep America Beautiful
1010 Washington Boulevard
Stamford, CT 06901
(203) 659-3000
Email: info@kab.org
http://www.kab.org

National Waste and Recycling Association
1550 Crystal Drive, suite 804
Arlington, VA 22202
(800) 424-2869; (202) 244-4700
Email: info@wasterecycling.org
https://wasterecycling.org

Bibliography

Aguirre, Itziar. "Cairo's 'Zabaleen' Garbage Collectors: Egypt's Diamond in the Rough." *Global Risk Insights*, June 12, 2015. http://globalriskinsights.com/2015/06/cairos-zabaleen-garbage-collectors-egypts-diamond-in-the-rough.

Ahmed, Syed Farez. "The Global Cost of Electronic Waste." *Atlantic*, September 29, 2016. http://www.theatlantic.com/technology/archive/2016/09/the-global-cost-of-electronic-waste/502019.

Association of Science–Technology Centers. "The Rotten Truth: A Garbage Timeline." Accessed March 18, 2017. http://www.astc.org/exhibitions/rotten/timeline.htm.

Barboza, David. "China's 'Queen of Trash' Finds Riches in Waste Paper." *New York Times*, January 15, 2007. http://www.nytimes.com/2007/01/15/business/worldbusiness/15iht-trash.4211783.html.

Bradbury, Matt. "A Brief Timeline of the History of Recycling." Busch Systems. May 20, 2014. http://www.buschsystems.com/resource-center/page/a-brief-timeline-of-the-history-of-recycling.

European Commission Joint Research Center. "Lifestyle Thinking and Assessment for Waste Management." http://eplca.jrc.ec.europa.eu/uploads/waste-waste-LCA-LCT.pdf.

European Environment Agency. "Recycling Rates in Europe." June 20, 2013. http://www.eea.europa.eu/about-us/competitions/waste-smart-competition/recycling-rates-in-europe/view.

Greenpeace. "History and Successes." http://www.greenpeace.org/international/en/about/history.

Grossman, David. "The 2020 Olympics Medals Will Be Made of Recycled Phones." *Popular Mechanics*, February 1, 2017. http://www.popularmechanics.com/technology/design/a25012/olympic-medals-recycled-phones.

Hutchinson, Alex. "Is Recycling Worth It? PM Investigates Its Economic and Environmental Impact." *Popular Mechanics*, November 12, 2008. http://www.popularmechanics.com/science/environment/a3752/4291566.

Makower, Joel. "The Closed Loop Fund, at Age Two, Goes with the Flow." *GreenBiz*, November 14, 2016. http://www.greenbiz.com/article/closed-loop-fund-age-two-goes-flow.

Malone, Robert. "World's Worst Waste." *Forbes*, May 24, 2006. http://www.forbes.com/2006/05/23/waste-worlds-worst-cx_rm_0524waste.html.

Natural Resources Defense Council. "The Story of *Silent Spring*." August 13, 2015. http://www. nrdc.org/stories/story-silent-spring.

Organisation for Economic Co-operation and Development. *Environment at a Glance 2015: OECD Indicators*. Paris, France: OECD Publishing, 2015. doi:10.1787/9789264235199-en.

Shegerian, John. "The Impact of the Reuse Movement with Community Recycling's Ira Baseman." *Green Is Good* podcast. November 21, 2014. https:// greenisgoodshow.com/episode/2014/11/impact-reuse-movement-community-recycling-ira-baseman.

Tucker, Booth. *The Social Relief Work of the Salvation Army in the United States*. Albany, NY: J. B. Lyon, 1900.

United Nations. *UN Conference on Environment and Development (1992)*. May 23, 1997. http://www. un.org/geninfo/bp/enviro.html.

United Nations Global Development Research Center. *Key Facts on Waste Issues*. http://www. gdrc.org/uem/waste/key-facts.html.

United Nations Sustainable Development. *United Nations Conference on Environment and Development, Rio de Janeiro, Brazil, 3 to 14 June 1992: Agenda 21*. https://sustainabledevelopment.un.org/ content/documents/Agenda21.pdf.

United States Environmental Protection Agency. "Advancing Sustainable Materials Management: 2014 Fact Sheet." November 2016. http://www.epa.gov/sites/production/files/2016-11/documents/2014_smmfactsheet_508.pdf.

United States Environmental Protection Agency. "Municipal Solid Waste." March 29, 2016. https://archive.epa.gov/epawaste/nonhaz/municipal/web/html.

Waring, George E., Jr. "The Cleaning of a Great City." *McClure's*, April 1987. http://brooklynrail.org/2012/03/local/the-cleaning-of-a-great-city.

Index

Page numbers in **boldface** are illustrations. Entries in **boldface** are glossary terms.

mercury, 62

methane, 44, 51, 55

Mobro 4000, 38–39, **42**

Nelson, Gaylord, 23, 25, 28

Nine Dragons Paper, 78–79

nitrous oxide, 55

Nixon, Richard, 28

nonrenewable resource, 54–55, 57, 70

nuclear tests, 26–27

oil spills, 22–23, **24**, 25, 33

organic waste, 44, 49, 96

packaging, 38, 45, 49–50, 59–60, **76**, 79

Paduh, Bojan, 66–67

paper, 9, 12–14, 16, 29, 39, 43–44, 46, 49, 54, 56, 70, 75, **76**, 78–81, 88, 96

pesticides, 20, 22, 33

PET, 57, 59

picking yards, 14

planned obsolescence, 61

plastic, 18, 39, 43, 46, 56–57, 59–60, 62, 75, 77, 80–81, 83, 85, 91, **92**, 93

product design, 9, 50–51, 57, 83, 89, 93, 95

PVC, 57, 59

pyrolysis, 93

recovery, 83, 87, **88**, 89, 91

recycling

    challenges, 74–75, 77, 80–81

    facilities, 8–9, 13, 39, 43, **52**, 60, **67**, 71, 75, 80–81, **82**, **90**

    history of, 12–14, 16, 30–31, 37–39, 43, 45, 49, 74–75, 77–78

    laws, 8, 28, 30–31, 45, 49, 57

    practices today, 46–47, **48**, 49–51, **52**, 55–57, 59–62, 64, 69–71, 77, 79–81, 83–86, **90**, 91, 93, 95–99, **99**

    statistics, 13, **19**, 30, 38–39, 43, 46–47, 49, 54–56, 60–61, 75, 77, 80–81, 93, 97

    symbol, **6**, 28–29, 45, 49, 59

Recycling Council of Ontario, 84–85

reduce, 5–9, 37–38, 44–45, 49–51, 69–71, 84, 91, 93

renewable energy, 89, 96

resin identification code, 59

Resource Conservation and Recovery Act, 28

About the Author

Ann Byers did not realize how many different connections she had with the subject of recycling until she started research for this book. She lives in Fresno, California, which is one of the top cities in the country for recycling, diverting 73 percent of its waste from landfills. And, speaking of Fresno and landfills, the city was home to the first modern, sanitary landfill in the United States, which opened in 1937. Long before moving to California, Byers lived in University City, Missouri, a suburb of St. Louis, which was one of the first municipalities in the country to offer curbside recycling to its residents. Despite her history with recycling, she still has trouble remembering to take her reusable bags to the grocery store in compliance with California's ban on plastic bags.